DAILY LIFE IN
THE INCA
EMPIRE

DAILY LIFE IN

THE INCA EMPIRE

MICHAEL A. MALPASS

The Greenwood Press "Daily Life Through History" Series

GREENWOOD PRESS
Westport, Connecticut • London

Library of Congress Cataloging-in-Publication Data

Malpass, Michael Andrew.
    Daily life in the Inca empire / Michael A. Malpass.
        p.   cm. — (The Greenwood Press "Daily life through history"
    series, ISSN 1080–4749)
    Includes bibliographical references and index.
    ISBN 0–313–29390–2 (alk. paper)
    1. Incas. I. Title. II. Series.
    F3429.M26   1996
    984'.01—dc20   95–44699

British Library Cataloguing in Publication Data is available.

Copyright © 1996 by Michael A. Malpass

All rights reserved. No portion of this book may be
reproduced, by any process or technique, without the
express written consent of the publisher.

Library of Congress Catalog Card Number: 95–44699
ISBN: 0–313–29390–2
ISSN: 1080–4749

First published in 1996

Greenwood Press, 88 Post Road West, Westport, CT 06881
An imprint of Greenwood Publishing Group, Inc.

Printed in the United States of America

The paper used in this book complies with the
Permanent Paper Standard issued by the National
Information Standards Organization (Z39.48–1984).

10 9 8 7 6 5 4 3 2

To my parents,
Leslie and Winona Malpass,
for their love and support through the years.

Contents

Preface

The Incas created the largest empire ever in the western hemisphere prior to the coming of Europeans in the sixteenth century. The Incas conquered much of western South America in less than a century, subjugating a wide variety of cultures ranging from small farming societies to very large, urban ones. How the Incas dominated this area is the subject of this book. However, the Incas were more than conquest armies and military leaders; they included people from many walks of life. Most books about the Incas typically focus on the ruling class and its accomplishments. This book attempts to look beyond the ruling class and give a general description of the way of life of other members of Inca society as well. A particularly distinct contribution of this book is its separate descriptions of the Inca way of life in the capital of Cuzco, and the way of life of their conquered subjects. This distinction allows the reader to understand how the Incas were both unique and typical of other Andean societies of the time. It also allows the reader to see how the Incas were able to manipulate various aspects of their subjects' lives for their own purposes.

In addition, the book includes more of a female perspective than previous books. Because many early sources that are used to describe the Inca way of life were written by men, there may be an unconscious bias toward the activities of men in the literature on the Incas. More recent books, such as Irene Silverblatt's *Moon, Sun, and Witches* (1987), have attempted to remedy the situation by focusing on women's roles. This book tries to present a more balanced view of male and female contributions to Inca and non-Inca culture.

Regarding the book's organization, the Introduction describes the basic sources of information about the Incas, pointing out how certain limitations to this information affect what is known about them. The Introduction also provides a general overview of the Incas and their empire, discussing the nature of their civilization, how the empire developed, and who the important figures were. In addition, it explains the historical chronology of the Incas.

Chapter 1 introduces the area encompassed by the Inca empire. The first part describes the geography of the Inca empire, reviewing the range of environmental conditions within it. The second part discusses pre-Inca cultural developments. This information places the Incas in a historical perspective, showing how they were both similar to and unique from the cultures that came before them.

Chapter 2 examines the political, social, and economic organization of the Inca empire, as well as the technological accomplishments for which the Incas are so famous. Chapter 3 provides more personal details about the daily lives of individuals. Here the distinction between the Incas' private lives and those of their subjects provides interesting contrasts. Chapter 4 discusses the nature of science in the Inca empire and explains the different calendars they used. Chapter 5 explores Inca religion. Because religion was so pervasive in Inca daily life, the discussion treats in greater detail some of the facets of Inca life that were introduced in earlier chapters.

Chapter 6 presents the author's reconstruction of a day in the life of an Inca family in Cuzco, and a day in a conquered family's life. These reconstructions are an attempt to provide a sense of what the daily life in the Inca empire might have been like. Of course one can never know how individuals were feeling; but given the commonality of emotions such as love for family and homeland, one can imagine how individuals might have reacted to the conditions under which they lived. The various activities and ideas presented in these reconstructions exemplify in a more personal way the information presented in the previous chapters.

Chapter 7 surveys the Inca contributions to modern Andean society and to the rest of the world. The discussion takes up the history of the empire after the Spanish Conquest, to show how modern Andean society is a product of both its pre-Hispanic and its European roots. The reader will learn that much of the Inca way of life still exists in the Andean countryside today, as a result of the effectiveness of that way of life.

Chapter 8 addresses the present crisis over the destruction of archaeological sites worldwide. Much of what is known about the Incas—and all that is known about most of the cultures that preceded them—has been learned through archaeology. Yet the destruction of many sites of ancient societies means that the possibility of losing all these sources is real and immediate. The chapter offers suggestions about how the crisis might be overcome and what individuals can do to help.

For the ease of the reader, a glossary of Inca terms used in this book is included. An explanation of the spelling of Inca terms is also necessary, as there is a trend today in Inca studies to use traditional Quechua (the language of the Incas and many modern Peruvians) forms. For example, using the Quechua forms the word *Inca* would be spelled *Inka,* and *quipu* would be *khipo.* However, because the Spanish forms are more recognizable to the lay reader, they are used here.

Books are the products of collaboration between individuals, and this one is no different. Even though the author did the actual writing of the text, many others contributed in different ways. In addition to those who provided illustrations, Brian Bauer, an authority on the archaeology of the Cuzco region, provided helpful clarification concerning aspects of Inca social and political organization. Any fuzzy thinking that remains is entirely the author's. Fred Estabrook of Ithaca College produced the map and provided the excellent photographs of all the illustrations. Thomas Longin, Provost of Ithaca College, funded the production of the illustrations and covered other fees associated with them. The author was granted a reduced teaching load by Howard Erlich, Dean of the School of Humanities and Sciences at Ithaca College, to provide the needed time to complete the manuscript in the spring of 1995. Barbara Rader, Desirée Bermani, and the competent staff at Greenwood Publishing Group brought the book to fruition and were understanding of the author's delays and problems along the way. Barbara's critical eye also prompted many helpful changes in the early draft of the book, which resulted in the more polished version seen here.

Finally, the author acknowledges a special note of gratitude to his wife, Susanne Kessemeier, for the encouragement and support without which this book would not have been finished. She also provided welcome advice on Chapter 6. Soren, our son, was unquestionably an inspiration, as well as an occasional frustration!

Historical Timeline of the Inca Empire

The history of the Incas is known only through oral traditions, since they had no written records. Because of this, it is very difficult to assess the truth of the histories given by the Incas. In addition, as will be discussed in greater detail in the Introduction, it is uncertain how well the early Spaniards understood the Incas' concepts of time and history. Nonetheless, according to the Spanish sources most often cited, there had been thirteen Inca kings. The following is a list of them, in order of rule.

1. Manco Capac
2. Sinchi Roca
3. Lloque Yupanqui
4. Mayta Capac
5. Capac Yupanqui
6. Inca Roca
7. Yahuar Huacac
8. Viracocha Inca
9. Pachacuti Inca Yupanqui
10. Topa Inca Yupanqui
11. Huayna Capac
12. Huascar
13. Atahuallpa

With the exception of the last four, the lengths of the reigns of the Inca kings are uncertain; in fact, it is not really clear whether the earlier kings were even real, or were mythical. In addition, there was a king who ruled briefly between Viracocha Inca and Pachacuti Inca Yupanqui named Inca Urcon. However, his name was officially removed from the list by his successor, Pachacuti, who claimed the kingship as his right after saving Cuzco from a siege by enemies (see Introduction).

Archaeology has confirmed that the Incas can be identified by their *artifacts* (any object made or modified by humans) as early as A.D. 1200 in the vicinity of Cuzco. It is probable that the first eight kings, if they did exist, were local leaders, who restricted their military activities to the region around Cuzco. The first expansion of the Incas outside of their homeland began in A.D. 1438. The following is a chronology of the major events in the development of the Inca empire.

early 1400s (?)	The Incas living around Cuzco defeat nearby groups and incorporate them into their society. The Incas ally themselves with the Lupaca, a powerful society living near Lake Titicaca, to assure no attack from that direction.
1438	Chanca tribe attacks the Incas from the north. The eighth king, Viracocha Inca, and his chosen heir to the throne, Inca Urcon, flee Cuzco. Another son, Inca Yupanqui, leads Incas to victory over the Chanca. Inca Yupanqui takes the name of Pachacuti and claims the kingship.
1438–1463	Under Pachacuti Inca Yupanqui, the Incas conquered the highland area between Lake Titicaca in the south and Lake Junín in the north.
1463	Pachacuti remains king, but turns over the control of the army to his son, Topa Inca. The latter extends the empire to just north of modern-day Quito, Ecuador, including all the coastal and highland regions of northern and central Peru.
1471	Topa Inca becomes king. Over the next 22 years, he expands the empire's southern boundaries to south-central Chile, including large areas of modern highland Bolivia and northwest Argentina. He also conquers the southern coastal region of Peru.

1493	Huayna Capac becomes king. Between A.D. 1493–1525, he completes the expansion of the empire to the limits seen on the map (p. xxiv). Essentially, he pushes the northern borders to the modern Ecuadorian–Colombian boundary, and annexes an area in the jungles of eastern Peru near Cajamarca.
1527	Huayna Capac dies suddenly, without naming an heir to replace him. Two rivals, Huascar and Atahuallpa, claim the kingship, starting a civil war that lasts five years.
1532	Atahuallpa's armies defeat Huascar's, making the former the uncontested king. The Spaniards arrive on the north coast, and capture Atahuallpa in Cajamarca. They hold him for ransom, then kill him. A puppet ruler is installed as king.
1537	The most serious rebellion against Spanish rule, led by Manco Inca, is put down, ending serious resistance to Spanish rule.

Introduction

Who were the Incas? What enabled them to build the vast empire that existed in the sixteenth century when the Europeans arrived in South America? What kind of empire was it? What distinguished the Inca empire from other cultures and civilizations? These questions are the focus of this chapter. But where do we find information to answer these questions? A discussion of the basic sources of information will show how our knowledge concerning the Incas is limited, and how this can lead to uncertainties about aspects of their lives and empire.

SOURCES OF INFORMATION

Two basic sources allow us to reconstruct the Inca way of life: historical documents and archaeology. Both provide distinctive kinds of information. But both have important drawbacks, so one must carefully weigh what is fact and what is educated opinion. A third source of information is contemporary Andean people. In some instances they appear to be living a way of life not far removed from that of their Inca and pre-Inca ancestors.

The Incas had no writing system of their own. Nonetheless, historical information about the Incas is available to researchers because the early Spaniards wrote documents about them. These documents include accounts of the Spanish conquest of the Incas by the members of the army; records by Spanish officials who tried to organize the conquered people for taxation purposes; Catholic Church records; legal documents concerning court action

Historical Documents

brought by the Incas during the Colonial Period; and letters from both Spanish and native writers, such as Cieza de León and Guaman Poma. Some of the records are invaluable because they present firsthand information about the Inca empire as seen by Spanish writers. Some are important because they were written by Incas or their immediate descendants, thus passing down the actual Inca point of view. Indeed, the historical record provides a wealth of information about how the Incas actually lived and how their empire was organized.

However, there are drawbacks to using the historical record (Malpass 1993a: 6–7). First, the Spanish writers were describing activities and institutions that were very different from their own, but they often described Inca culture in terms of their own society. As an example, consider the list of kings given by the Incas. As presented in the historical chronology, Spanish sources indicate there were thirteen kings who ruled sequentially. The names were given to them by Inca informants. However, one school of thought in Inca studies suggests that the names were not actual people but, rather, titles filled by different individuals (Zuidema 1983). Thus the number of actual kings may have been fewer, and several titles may have been filled at the same time. The early Spanish writers, being unfamiliar with such a system of titles, simply translated it into something they *were* familiar with: a succession of kings. Given that the Inca empire expanded only during the time of the last four kings, or as a result of the actions of the individuals in those four positions, this question is not deemed significant for an understanding of the Incas. But the example shows that biases and inaccuracies may have been introduced inadvertently from the very beginning of the written Spanish reports about the Incas. Moreover, early writers often copied information from each other—so misinformation was likely to be passed on and accepted as true by later scholars (Rowe 1946: 193).

Second, both Spanish and Inca writers sometimes had motives for being deliberately deceitful. For example, in an effort to gain status in the Spaniards' eyes, a native person might say that he formerly had been more important in the Inca empire than he actually was. Spanish officials were occasionally untruthful when it served their purposes as well. For example, a Spaniard might deliberately underreport the productivity of a region under his authority so he could sell the additional products and keep the money, rather than hand it over to the Spanish Crown.

Third, it should be noted that the Spaniards' main sources of information were the Incas themselves, often members of the Inca ruling class. Therefore, what was recorded was the Incas' point of view about their own history and empire. Some modern authorities question whether the history of the Incas happened as they said it did (Bauer 1992; Urton 1990;

Zuidema 1990). Although some of their history is certainly more myth than truth—they were said to have originated in caves—many, if not most, scholars agree that the history of the last four Inca kings is probably accurate. The same is true of other things told to the Spanish: the more recently an event is said to have occurred, the more likely it is to have actually happened.

A fourth problem relates to the nature of the Inca conquests and how accurate the accounts of those conquests are—whether related by the Spaniards or by the Incas on whom they relied. It was certainly in the Incas' interest to describe themselves as invincible and just. However, lacking accounts by conquered people about their interactions with the Incas, it is unknown how much of the Inca conquest as related by the ruling class is factual.

Finally, there is a certain vagueness in the historical record regarding places and names. Many Spanish writers listed places they had visited within the empire, including both provinces and towns. However, other writers traveling along the same routes sometimes recounted different lists of places. In addition, it is difficult to identify the exact locations of towns and other geographic points of reference because of the widespread movements of people over the past five centuries. These problems make it difficult for modern researchers to verify information in the historical record.

For all these reasons, the historical record must be carefully evaluated to determine whether it is accurate and to verify the locations of past events. One approach is to cross-check information from a number of authors. Another approach is to conduct archaeological research. Regardless of the problems, historical documents provide a wealth of exceptional information about the Incas.

In terms of written sources of information, one must distinguish between primary sources and secondary sources. Primary sources are first-hand accounts about the Incas, such as the record of the conquest and the observations of the first Spanish administrators, clergy, and others. Perhaps the most famous primary source on the Incas is Felipe Guaman Poma de Ayala's *El Primer Nueva Corónica y Buen Gobierno*. This book was actually a 1,100-page letter written between 1584–1615 to the King of Spain, protesting the treatment of the Andean natives by the Spaniards. Guaman Poma was a native of Huánuco in the northern highlands. Not only did he offer exceptional detail about Inca life, but he included 398 drawings to illustrate his information. Most of the illustrations used in this book are from Guaman Poma's work.

Secondary sources draw on primary ones, coordinating and compiling information from different documents. Both primary and secondary sources can be subject to the problems mentioned above, so neither is necessarily better than the other. In this book, two secondary sources

CAMÍNA EL AVTOR

Guaman Poma's drawing of himself as he
traveled around Peru.

of information about the Incas are frequently cited. The first is Father
Bernabé Cobo's *Inca Religion and Customs,* the English version of which
was published in 1990. Cobo was a Spanish priest who came to Peru
in 1599. His book was part of a much larger work entitled *Historia del
Nuevo Mundo,* which was published in Spain in 1653. The religion section is one of the best sources on Inca religion, because it uses primary
sources that are lost. Its detail is extraordinary, providing many facts
about the Inca religion that were not noted by other writers. The second source is John H. Rowe's *Inca Culture at the Time of the Spanish
Conquest,* published in 1946. This classic essay, an exhaustive description of the Incas, uses many of the early Spanish sources (which are all
in Spanish), including Cobo. Rowe provides not only an excellent account but a clear statement of the drawbacks and ambiguities inherent
in his sources. For many aspects of Inca culture, this essay remains the

best. However, much new information has become available that modifies or replaces what was known in 1946, such as that found in *Inka Settlement Planning* (1990) by John Hyslop, or Irene Silverblatt's *Moon, Sun, and Witches* (1987).

The second major source of information about the Incas is *archaeology*, a set of techniques and procedures for reconstructing past cultures on the basis of their remains. **Archaeology** Archaeologists carefully dig up the tools, food remains, houses, and other aspects of past societies, then use many kinds of analyses to evaluate and interpret the remains. This information is fundamentally different from the kind provided by historical documents, because it provides details about the uses of different sites, the tools they used, how their towns were laid out, and where people conducted various activities.

Archaeology too has drawbacks. First, not all of a society's activities leave objects that can be discovered later. For example, religious beliefs, languages, and marriage patterns do not necessarily leave any remains. Second, of the social activities for which objects or structures *do* remain, nature has a tendency to destroy many that are not made of durable materials. It is rare to find objects of wood, bone, cloth, or animal fibers because they decompose. (In the case of Peru and Chile, the dry coast actually preserves many of these objects, allowing archaeologists to recover much more than in other areas of the world. In contrast, many objects are destroyed by natural processes in the wet highlands.) Third, humans themselves sometimes destroy the remains of past cultures, both deliberately and accidentally. This problem is the focus of the final chapter of the book.

In sum, using both historical records and archaeology enables us to gain a more complete picture of the Incas than either source can provide alone. Archaeology can verify and amplify the historical accounts, and documents can provide information not visible in the archaeological record. For example, historical records indicate that a particular group of natives from Andamarca, a region in central Peru, served as the official people who carried the Inca king in a litter and that this was the only service they provided to the empire. Archaeologists would never be able to "dig up" or confirm this information about the Andamarcans as litter bearers; yet archaeological research has indicated that the Andamarcans also produced food for the empire, a fact not recorded in the historical documents (Schreiber 1993).

Unfortunately, there are few historical documents about the people who lived before the Incas. Therefore, all our information about earlier cultures must come from archaeology. With careful study and interpretation, however, much can be inferred about these societies.

Members of the Inca nobility using the
Andean footplow for breaking up soil prior
to planting.

**Contemporary
Andean People**

A final source of information about the Inca past is the study of contemporary Andean people. Because of the difficult terrain in the Andes, many remote areas have changed little since Inca times. For example, traditional agriculture makes use of many of the same tools as the Incas used, such as the footplow. Studying how people live today can sometimes help interpret archaeological information. Traditional ways of life also serve as models for comparison to the historical and archaeological records.

THE INCAS

The Incas as a distinct group can be documented archaeologically from A.D. 1200. It is clear that they were only one of many small ethnic groups living in the mountains of southern Peru throughout most of their history. In fact, as will be discussed in more detail in Chapter 1, they were not even the largest or most powerful political group in the Andean region during most of the time they existed. Their conquests of neighboring people began in A.D. 1438, as a result of an invasion of their territory by a rival society. This catalyst set in motion the development of the Inca empire, which lasted until they were conquered by the Spaniards in A.D. 1532.

Why did the Incas expand their authority as far as they did? They could just as well have repulsed the invaders and remained a small society. The question of how and why the Incas built their empire will be addressed here.

Little is known of the Incas' first eight kings; they existed so far back in time that accounts of their reigns were unverifiable by the Spaniards and later scholars. The origin myth of the Incas states that their founders came from a town south of Cuzco called Pacariqtambo. There, four brothers and four sisters came out of a cave. These eight were the ancestors of the Inca kings. The main figure of the four men was Manco Capac, who became the first king. Other people came out of two nearby caves, and the eight Incas gathered them together and set off in search of a place to settle. When they arrived at the site of Cuzco, they drove out the people who were living there and founded their own capital. The subsequent kings were descendants of Manco Capac; the other Incas were descendants of the people recruited at Pacariqtambo. (This myth is discussed in more detail in Chapter 5.) Oral accounts of the deeds of the later kings were recorded by the Spaniards.

It is possible that the early kings were real individuals but that their exploits were exaggerated to make them appear more impressive. Equally likely is that the early kings were mythical, made up to account for the origin of the Incas—and perhaps to justify their positions as rulers (Urton 1990: Ch. 2). By the 1300s and early 1400s, warfare between rival ethnic groups all over the Andes had become widespread. By the middle of the fifteenth century, the Incas had conquered several of the formerly independent societies that lived adjacent to them. This made the Incas a political force to be reckoned with.

To the south of the Incas in the region around Lake Titicaca, two powerful societies—the Lupaca and Colla—were a chief threat to the Incas, so both wished to gain the Incas as their allies. Although the Incas allied themselves with the Lupaca, after a great battle the Lupaca defeated the Colla without the Incas' help, thereby securing the southern border of Inca territory.

However, to the north the Incas' former neighbors, the Quechua, were defeated by another rival, the Chanca, who then began plans to attack the Incas. The Chanca waited until the ruler, Viracocha Inca, became elderly; then they attacked the Incas, driving them back to the capital of Cuzco. Viracocha and his appointed heir, Inca Urcon, fled the city, thinking it could not be saved. Others, however, including another

Map of Tahuantinsuyu, the Inca Empire

Modern cities and valleys mentioned in text

1. Cajamarca
2. Lima
3. Cuzco
4. Trujillo
5. Huánuco
6. Casma valley
7. Moche valley
8. Colca valley

Archaeological sites mentioned in text

9. Huánuco Pampa
10. El Paraiso
11. Salinas de Chao
12. La Galgada
13. Chavin de Huántar
14. Chiripa
15. Pucara
16. Tiahuanaco
17. Nazca
18. Huari
19. Arequipa
20. Chan Chan
21. Lake Junín

Bold dotted-and-dashed lines indicate borders of the four quarters of the empire. Underlined terms are the names of the four quarters (e.g., *Antisuyu*).

Dotted lines are major roads in the Inca system.

Solid lines indicate modern political borders.

of Viracocha's sons, Inca Yupanqui, stayed to defend the city. Yupanqui became commander and called on the Incas' allies to come to their aid. When the Chanca attacked the city, they were repulsed. At a critical point in the battle Yupanqui is said to have called out that even the stones in the fields were turning into men to help them. These stones were carefully collected after the battle and placed in shrines as sacred objects.

After the battle for Cuzco, the Incas and their allies continued counterattacking the Chanca until the latter were soundly defeated. Yupanqui claimed the throne from his brother Inca Urcon and added "Pachacuti" to his name, which means "earthquake" or "cataclysm" in the Inca language. The defeat of the Chanca made the Incas a much more powerful group than before, as they required the Chanca to serve in their army. Over the next 25 years, Pachacuti extended the empire farther north to the region around Lake Junín, located east of modern-day Lima. He also conquered the Incas' former rivals, the Lupaca and Colla, who were becoming rebellious as a result of the increased power of the Incas.

In A.D. 1463, after the Lake Titicaca campaigns, Pachacuti turned over control of the Inca armies to his son and heir, Topa Inca, and focused his energies on the organization of the empire and the reorganization of Cuzco, the Inca capital. Topa Inca began a series of successful wars in the highlands that extended the empire to present-day Quito. He then reversed direction and marched down the coast of Peru, conquering the powerful Chimu and other societies in that region. Eventually he brought the entire coastal area from Ecuador to south of Nazca into the empire.

In A.D. 1471, Pachacuti formally turned the kingship over to Topa Inca, who began his reign by attacking groups living on the eastern side of the Andes in the area that drops into the Amazonian tropical forest. This campaign was ended abruptly by another rebellion by the Lupaca and Colla, who had heard that the Incas had suffered a defeat by the tropical forest groups and so were weakened. Topa Inca proved them wrong by soundly defeating them and their allies, thereby extending the Inca empire into Bolivia. He then pushed on into northwestern Argentina and invaded Chile from the east. He stopped at the banks of the Maule River in south-central Chile, apparently unable or unwilling to fight the fierce Araucanian groups who lived further south.

Topa Inca died in A.D. 1493 and was succeeded by his son, Huayna Capac. This king spent most of his reign in Quito and greatly expanded the importance of that city to the Incas. He also expanded the empire slightly farther north and conquered several groups on the flanks of the Andes east of Cajamarca. Thus the Inca empire reached its greatest extension by A.D. 1525, a mere 87 years after Pachacuti began his conquests.

What enabled the Incas to establish the greatest empire of the New World? Most scholars agree it was a combination of outstanding military organization and effective administration of conquered peoples. The Incas had superb generals who were able to defeat their enemies consistently. In addition, after the defeat of the Chancas, the Incas had an army that was simply larger than any rival army. In an area where battles were won or lost by hand-to-hand combat, having more soldiers was a key to ensuring victory.

Equally important was the administration of the conquered regions. The Incas were able to integrate the conquered groups into their empire effectively by minimizing changes while maximizing productivity. How they achieved this is discussed in Chapter 2.

Another key to the Incas' success was their policy of moving people to fit the needs of the state. The Incas moved whole villages of people, sometimes over long distances. There are reports of Ecuadorian people being moved to Bolivia. This policy enabled the Incas to increase crop yields in regions that were underproductive. It also had the advantage of keeping rebellious people under control.

Even though the military and administrative skills of the Incas explain *how* the Incas were able to build their empire, they do not explain *why* the Incas conquered such a large area. As stated previously, it wasn't necessary for the Incas to continue conquering groups after they repulsed the Chanca attack; they could have returned to their original borders and continued their lives as before. No one has provided a reason for the Inca conquests that is generally accepted as correct. It is likely that several factors were important. One of the most important was the strong emphasis on being a warrior in Inca society. Much of a boy's upbringing was focused on developing traits that would serve him well as a warrior.

But why the emphasis on being a warrior? No doubt this was influenced by the times during which the Inca culture developed. The period immediately preceding the expansion of the Incas is characterized as a time of conflict throughout the Andes. Warfare and raiding were common between societies and even between rival towns. Such conditions would favor the development of warriors as an important part of society, for protection as well as for conquest.

Another possible factor was the political ambitions of the Inca kings. Perhaps Pachacuti became obsessed with the idea of ruling the known world, so he continued the expansion of the empire for personal gain. His taking of the name Pachacuti might support this suggestion. His ambitions might have been passed down to his son and heir, Topa Inca, and thence to his grandson, Huayna Capac.

Another possibility has been suggested by Geoffrey Conrad and Arthur Demarest—an Andean scholar and a specialist in Mexican archaeology, respectively. They suggest it was the Incas' religious beliefs, coupled with environmental factors, that led them to the conquest. The Incas practiced a pattern of inheritance that left the land and wealth of a king to all his descendants except his heir; the new king had to find his own source of wealth. This was based in religion: the Incas believed their kings never died but were divine rulers, so their lands and wealth remained under their authority forever. As the land near Cuzco was taken by successive kings, later ones had to find their own lands further and further away, until it became necessary to conquer other people to obtain it. Conquest became a means to obtain additional wealth, which remained with the family of the king who achieved it. Pressure would have been placed on the new king to gain as much as his father did for his family, thereby requiring even more conquests even farther away. Although this is an intriguing possibility, it doesn't explain why Huayna Capac, the eleventh king, conquered such a limited area.

It will probably never be known with certainty why the Incas expanded their empire to the extent they did. It is likely that several factors played a role. The early crisis precipitated by the Chanca attack might have led to the initial expansion as a result of the perceived need to defeat the Chanca as completely as possible. Also, it is possible that Pachacuti and Topa Inca were simply ambitious and power-hungry men. Given that most members of the Inca society benefited in some way from the conquests, it is easy to envision how Inca society might have supported the further conquests. Religious specialists, the priests and priestesses of Inca religion, certainly would have been supportive: they were the recipients of much of the wealth that came to Cuzco from conquered regions. Inca religion might therefore have been the justification for the Incas' emergence as an Andean superpower.

Regardless of the reasons for the Inca conquests, what is particularly impressive is how many people were brought into their empire. Although population figures are difficult to determine, a figure of 10 million is not unreasonable (Cook 1981). However, this number reflects the total number of subjects in the empire. The Incas themselves, the group who originated in the vicinity of Cuzco, probably numbered around 40,000. That this group could subjugate millions of others is a credit to the military effectiveness of the Incas and their ability to organize and control their subjects.

THE INCA ACHIEVEMENT

What is distinctive about Inca civilization? Certainly their monumental building activities are one of the accomplishments for which they are most famous. They are perhaps best known as highly skilled stoneworkers, able to construct buildings of massive stones that were so well fitted together that a knife blade will not squeeze between them, even after over 400 years of earthquakes. And the Incas used neither cement nor mortar!

Other engineering feats are also part of the Inca legacy. Their ability to construct extensive systems of agricultural fields that resemble staircases going up the sides of mountains allowed for the production of huge amounts of food to feed themselves and the people who worked for them. The Incas built long irrigation canals to ensure that there would be adequate water for the crops. Many of the fields used by Andean farmers today were originally built by conquered people under Inca supervision, and many others are now abandoned. It is noteworthy that there are more abandoned fields in the Peruvian Andes today than ones in use (Denevan 1987); this suggests that populations were high during Inca times. This is certainly a tribute to the Incas' ability to produce large amounts of food.

Among other engineering marvels, the Inca road system stands out for its sheer size: over 14,000 miles of road were built. Although the road was not paved in the sense that modern ones are, it was carefully prepared to match the needs of the terrain through which it passed. In swampy areas it was raised with earth; in desert zones it was delineated with lines of stones. Along the road were centers and inns to cater to the needs of travellers. Bridges were built to cross rivers and stairways were cut to rise up steep hillsides.

The Incas are also known for their pottery. Both the shapes and the designs are distinctive. Probably the most typical Inca pot is the *aryballos*, a large storage vessel with pointed base and long flaring neck (see Figure on page 45). Such vessels were generally decorated with patterns of small triangles resembling feathers. Other typical pottery includes plates and vessels for serving liquids. The uniformity in Inca pottery is due to the fact that the Incas designed and used their pottery (and buildings as well) as a symbol of superiority over their subjects. Thus artifacts and structures were emblems of imperial power for all to see. They were standardized because they were produced at special manufacturing centers set up for just those purposes and made by skilled craftspeople. Other crafts, such as cloth and metal, were similarly organized.

According to early Spanish accounts, when they first saw it in A.D. 1533, Cuzco was an awe-inspiring city of many thousands of inhabitants. Under Pachacuti the city was remodeled and the two rivers that ran through it were straightened. Cuzco was said to be a model of the Inca empire. Incas lived in the city proper, while non-Incas, including people from all over the empire who were brought to the capital to work for the Incas, lived in separate settlements just outside the center of the city.

Perhaps the most enduring legacy of the Incas is the extent of change they brought to the groups they conquered. It was the Incas' goal to build an empire that was unified, to level the dramatic political and social differences that had existed between groups prior to the Inca expansion. To do this, they moved individuals and entire villages around the empire, breaking up larger societies and lumping smaller ones into administrative units of equal size. They introduced the Quechua language to their subjects, and it persists to this day as only one of two native languages still spoken in the area that was the Inca empire. As the noted Inca scholar John Rowe (1946: 329–330) has stated, the sense of common culture that millions of Andean people share today is more the result of the Incas' policies than those of the Spaniards. In fact, the Spaniards often merely continued the Inca policies. Thus it is difficult to say that the Incas no longer exist; as we discuss in Chapter 7, Inca culture is very much alive today—although in a modified form. This heritage is the greatest tribute to the Incas' impact on western South America.

1

Historical Overview

TAHUANTINSUYU: THE LAND OF THE FOUR QUARTERS

When the Spanish *conquistadores*, or conquerors, led by Francisco Pizarro, landed in northern Peru in A.D. 1532, they encountered an empire more vast than any previously known in the New World. The Incas called their empire Tahuantinsuyu, which in their native Quechua language meant "Land of the Four Quarters." The empire extended over a distance of 3,000 km (1,800 miles) from just south of the modern Colombian-Ecuadorian border to central Chile, and from the Pacific Ocean to the eastern foothills of the Andes Mountains. Included in this area was virtually every kind of environment, from the world's driest desert to steaming tropical forests, and from sea level to altitudes of over 7,000 m (23,100 ft). To understand the Incas and their way of life, one must first understand the nature of the land they controlled and the challenges it presented.

Tahuantinsuyu encompassed three distinct environments: the arid western coastal region, the Andean highlands, and the eastern Andean foothills. Each environment has a different climate and natural resources as well as distinct plant and animal communities. Long before the Incas, people adapted to these environments and learned to exploit the resources present in each. One of the challenges to the Incas was to integrate the diverse groups living in these environments into a single, unified empire.

**The
Arid
Coast**

The western coast of South America, from about the present border of Peru and Ecuador to central Chile, is an extremely dry desert. The dryness results from unique conditions that prohibit rain from falling. The Humboldt Current off the coast of this area brings cold water from the Antarctic regions up almost to the equator, before it veers west. The winds along the coast always blow onshore, cooling the air over the land. This results in relatively mild temperatures along the coast and little moisture that can rise, condense, and fall as rain. The Andes Mountains act as a barrier to prevent rain from reaching the coast from the east (Moseley 1975: 7–10).

During summer in the southern hemisphere (November–March) the coast heats up and the moist air from the sea rises up against the western slopes of the mountains. During this season the coastal weather is clear and warm, although it may be cloudy over the mountains. During the winter (May–October) the coast remains cool, so the moisture blowing onshore condenses near sea level and forms thick fog banks. Because northern Peru is close to the equator its climate is warmer, so the winter fog banks rise and may even break up during the day. However, after sunset they reform, making nights damp and foggy. Farther south, because it remains cool throughout the day, the fog lingers. In such a climatic situation, virtually no rain falls during any part of the year. Studies indicate that the coastal climate has been the same for at least the past 10,000 years.

The extreme aridity of the western coast results in the formation of a desert; in fact, the part of the coast that lies in southern Peru is the world's driest desert (Lettau and Lettau 1978). Unlike deserts in other parts of the world (e.g., the southwestern United States), there is not even sufficient moisture to support cactus. However, there are certain areas along the coast where unusual conditions allow sufficient moisture during the winter fogs to support some plants. These areas, or *lomas*, become more common and larger the farther south one goes, corresponding to the denser fog banks.

The dry coastal desert is broken periodically by rivers that flow down from the western flanks of the Andes. In Peru the rivers are approximately 40 km (24 miles) apart, but they become more widely separated in southern Peru and northern Chile. The coastal desert is much narrower in northern Peru than in southern Peru and Chile because the Andes are much closer to the Pacific Ocean in the north, becoming ever more distant from the coast as one goes south.

Where rivers flow down from the mountains, the valleys supported a dense growth of forest along their margins prior to the introduction of agriculture. Following the introduction of agriculture around 5,000 years ago (3,000 B.C.), the virgin forests began to be cut down. Irrigation became an important means of utilizing even more land for farming, start-

Coastal Peruvian desert.

ing around 3,800 years ago (1,800 B.C.). Now virtually all coastal valleys are farmed intensively, and little of the earlier forest is left.

The rivers are also important as the main sources of fresh water for the inhabitants of the coast. Although springs do appear occasionally in the desert, they are relatively scarce. Thus permanent human occupation of the coastal zone was restricted to the river valleys until the introduction of pumps by the Spaniards (after A.D. 1532). Even now, however, few coastal people live far away from the river valleys—except in the major cities (e.g., Lima and Arequipa), where water is provided by means of pipes.

In the northern part of Peru the river valleys are broad and wide, leaving very large areas that could be irrigated. In the southern part of the country the rivers cut more deeply into the landscape, so much less land can be irrigated. It is therefore no surprise that the prehistoric cultures of the northern coast were larger and more developed than those of the southern coast; more food could be grown in that area.

What the coast lacks in farmland it makes up for in fishing resources. The cold coastal waters support huge numbers of fish, shellfish, sea mammals, and sea birds. In fact, the ocean off Peru is one of the richest fishing zones in the world. This source of food became important early in the development of permanent settlements.

The Andean Highlands The second major environment in Tahuantinsuyu is the Andes Mountains. This environment is characterized by high mountain peaks and deep valleys. The Andes run the length of South America, from Colombia in the north to Tierra del Fuego at the southern tip of the continent. They are relatively narrow in northern Peru and Ecuador, forming two roughly parallel chains. In southern Peru, northern Chile, and Bolivia, the Andes reach their widest extent, being close to 640 km (400 miles) wide. The mountains again narrow in Chile to a single chain.

The height between peaks and valley bottoms in the Andes often exceeds 3,000 m (10,000 ft). Because of this enormous vertical distance, there is considerable variation in temperature and rainfall from the bottoms of the valleys to the tops of the mountains. In general the higher up one goes, the cooler and wetter the climate becomes; conversely, when one descends into a valley, the air becomes warmer and drier. Thus there are different zones of plants and animals, corresponding to particular combinations of rainfall and temperature. Most valleys have three main zones, called by their Quechua names *yunga, quechua,* and *puna* (Brush 1977: 9–10). The yunga zone is the lowest, lying below 1,500 m (5,000 ft); it is warm and dry. Plants that grow there include cactus, some fruit trees, and many thorny shrubs. With irrigation, many other plants can grow in this zone, including most food plants.

The quechua zone, lying between 1,500 and 3,500 m (5,000–11,500 ft), has always been productive for agriculture. This zone is higher than the yunga and lower than the puna, so it has intermediate temperatures and rainfall. Corn, beans, squash, fruit, and native crops such as *quinoa,* a protein-rich grain, do well in this zone. Prior to the introduction of agriculture, it is likely this zone was mostly forest (Brush 1977: 5); with the coming of agriculture, most of the native forests were cut down and converted to fields. In fact, most trees one sees in the Andes today are eucalyptus, which were imported from Australia starting in the nineteenth century.

The Cordillera Huayhuash in the Andean highlands.

The puna zone lies above the quechua zone (above 3,500 m) and is the highest zone of use to humans. It is characterized by cold temperatures and abundant rainfall. The zone is typically above the treeline, and the native plants are grasses. Only the lower parts of this zone can be used for agriculture, and then only for hardy, frost-resistant crops such as potatoes, *oca*, and *ullucu*, which are root crops native to highland South America. This high zone has traditionally been a major focus of food production (Brush 1977: 8).

The upper part of the puna is mostly used as pasture for the Andean peoples' herds of animals. Present-day farmers raise mostly cattle and sheep, but prior to the introduction of these animals by the Spaniards, *llamas* and *alpacas* were herded. The llama is slightly larger and is used as a beast of burden for carrying goods over the steep Andean terrain. The alpaca is smaller and is bred for its very fine wool, which is used in making warm clothing.

In contrast to farmers in the United States, who grow only a few kinds of any given plant, farming in the Andes emphasizes variety. Hundreds of varieties of corn and potatoes, the two most common native plants in Peru, are cultivated. For example, certain corn varieties have short cobs and relatively few kernels, whereas others are long and have many kernels—like that grown in the United States. The corn comes in many different colors, from yellow to white to purple. The same is true of potatoes and other root crops grown in the high quechua or low puna zones.

The varieties are not grown simply for their appearance; they are adapted to different conditions of rainfall, temperature, and pest resistance. They may also have different uses, such as for baking or boiling. In lower areas of the quechua zone, a farmer may grow one kind of corn that is resistant to drought; in areas higher up, he may grow another kind that is resistant to frost. In still other fields he may have other varieties that are resistant to different pests. By growing many different varieties with different characteristics, farmers can maximize food production by minimizing loss to natural factors.

Even though the three zones have the characteristics described above, it is important to note that the climate from year to year is highly variable in the highlands. In some years there may be abundant rainfall, making farming easier in the absence of irrigation. In other years there may be much less rainfall, making farming without irrigation difficult or impossible. The same is true for temperatures. Sometimes the frosts come early in the year or linger later, endangering the crops. For this reason, Andean farmers have developed strategies for dealing with the environmental uncertainties. In addition to growing a variety of crops, they cultivate fields in many different areas and grow different combinations of plants in each. Thus if one field is stricken by an early frost or suffers hail damage, other fields may be spared.

Farmers also use all three zones in different ways, depending on the distribution of the zones (Brush 1977: 10–16). In many valleys there is a large enough vertical distance from the valley bottom to the mountaintop for all three zones to be close together. In such circumstances people place their villages in the upper part of the quechua zone, to be close to their fields there and in the lower puna zones. But they may also have fields in the yunga zone. The distance to the fields in other zones may mean a walk of from one to several hours. For harvesting and planting in distant fields, farmers set up small huts and camp out for as many days as needed to complete their work there.

In some parts of the Andes, the different zones are spaced too far apart to be effectively used from a single village. In these regions a different pattern of zonal use developed whereby people specialized in the crops of the main zone, either the quechua or puna. They also had access to fields in the other zones, which may have been several days' journey from their home village. Three to four times a year they would travel to these more distant fields to plant and harvest the crops of that zone (Brush 1977: 13; Murra 1972).

In a variation on this last pattern, anthropologist John Murra (1975) suggests that some groups in the past actually sent members of their own community to live more or less permanently in the lower zones and produce the foods of those zones. Thus rather than traveling several times a year to the yunga zone, certain community members lived there instead. Products would be exchanged between community members in the different zones. Although these individuals may have lived permanently in a different area, they were still considered members of their community of birth.

There is yet another way by which people presently exploit the Andean highland area in regions where the mountains are not so steep (Brush 1977: 13–15). In these areas, people live in all the different zones but focus almost exclusively on the products of a single zone. Then they exchange the products with groups living in the other zones. Although this system is found primarily in the eastern and central Andes, another variant can be found in southeastern Peru and northwestern Bolivia. This area, which includes Lake Titicaca, is called the *Altiplano*, or high, flat plain. It is a vast region entirely within the puna zone. Here people grow puna products, then trade them with people who live in other zones to the east and west for the food produced in those zones. Caravans of llamas are used for carrying the produce down from the puna, sometimes as far as to the Pacific coast; then they return, bringing back the products of the yunga and quechua zones. The round-trip takes two months. It is likely that this pattern is an ancient one, having developed before the time of the Incas.

One final way by which some groups, notably the Incas, dealt with the environmental variability was by moving entire villages from one zone to another. This procedure, known by the Inca term *mitima*, was used to increase the amount of food produced in a given zone by moving whole groups of people into the zone. It is different from the pattern described previously, because the people usually were moved against their will as a result of the political policy of a dominant group. More will be said about mitimas in Chapter 2.

The third major environment encompassed by Tahuantinsuyu is the region where the high Andes decrease in altitude toward the east. In modern Peru and Ecuador, the Andes drop into the Amazonian lowlands to become a vast tropical rainforest. Here the foothills are called the *ceja de la montaña*, or **The Eastern Foothills** *ceja* for short. In Bolivia and Argentina, the Andes descend into flat, lowlying areas called the *Llanos de Mojos* and *Gran Chaco*, which are dry in the winter and flooded in the summer. Finally, in Argentina, the Andes drop into large grasslands called *pampas* which are similar to the Great Plains of the United States.

The Incas were a highland people, fully adapted to the climate and products of the highland zones. When they attempted to extend their empire into the eastern lowland regions, they had much less success, particularly when they invaded the tropical rainforests of Amazonia. The heat, humidity, dense vegetation, and guerrilla tactics of the groups living there made Inca warfare ineffective. Therefore, Tahuantinsuyu extended very little into this zone.

Nevertheless the ceja region of eastern Peru had economic importance to the Incas. In this environment of high rainfall and temperatures, certain tropical plants and animals are found—such as the *coca* plant—that were prized by the Incas. Coca was widely used by Andean people for chewing (much like tobacco), and it had great ceremonial significance to the Incas. Chewing coca reduces feelings of cold, fatigue, and thirst; thus it was helpful to farmers toiling in their fields in the highlands. Coca is still widely used for these purposes today (Hanna 1976).

Other products from the eastern foothills that were of value to highland people included colorful feathers from the birds that lived there, which were used in clothing. Some plants, such as *manioc* (a starchy root) and sweet potato, were first used in this region and then were introduced to the highlands and western coast. In fact, several important food crops of the Andean people may have had their origins in this region. The importance of the eastern foothills and tropical rainforest to Andean prehistory lies more in their contributions to earlier societies than in their economic importance to the Incas.

CHRONOLOGY OF THE PRE-INCA HISTORY OF THE CENTRAL ANDEAN REGION

Archaeologists and historians alike break up time into discrete units. Archaeologists divide time according to the appearance and disappearance of significant cultural developments, such as new tool types or ways of producing food. Many chronological schemes have been presented for the Andean region, but all document the same series of important cultural events. Unfortunately, the events occurred at different times in different areas, so any one scheme is hard to apply over the entire region of Tahuantinsuyu. Nevertheless, one scheme, the Rowe-Lanning chronology (named for John Rowe and Edward Lanning, the two archaeologists who developed it), is generally accepted and will be used as a point of reference in this chapter.

Western Andean prehistory can be divided into periods during which large areas were unified relatively quickly by some common cultural influence. In archaeological terms, this situation is called a *horizon*. The Rowe-Lanning scheme identifies three: the Early Horizon, Middle Horizon, and Late Horizon. Between these horizons were the Early Intermediate Period (which falls between the Early and Middle Horizons) and the Late Intermediate Period (which falls between the Middle and Late

Horizons). During the intermediate periods the integrating influences of the horizons broke down, and societies developed along individual lines. Two earlier periods are also identified: the Initial Period (which precedes the Early Horizon) and the Preceramic Period (which precedes the Initial Period). The Preceramic Period refers to the time before pottery was invented; it begins with the arrival of humans in South America. The Initial Period refers to the time when pottery first appeared.

This chronological scheme is best applied in the area of central Peru where it was developed. As one goes farther away from this region—into southern Peru, Chile, Bolivia, or Ecuador and Colombia—the periods have less utility because the cultural events on which they are based occurred at very different times, if at all. For the central Peruvian region, the dates and principal cultures of these periods are as follows:

Period	Date	Cultures
Preceramic Period	?–1800 B.C.	various local cultures
Initial Period	1800–900 B.C.	various local cultures
Early Horizon	900–200 B.C.	Chavin, Paracas
Early Intermediate Period	200 B.C.–A.D. 600	Moche, Nasca
Middle Horizon	A.D. 600–1000	Huari, Tiahuanaco
Late Intermediate Period	A.D. 1000–1438	Chimu, Chancay
Late Horizon	A.D. 1438–1532	Inca

It is important to briefly discuss the cultural developments that preceded the Incas in order to put their achievements into a historical perspective. Much of what the Incas accomplished was based on earlier cultures' activities, discoveries, and lifestyles. For example, the Incas relied on domesticated crops for their food. Yet the domestication process began during the Preceramic Period. Also, the Incas are famous for their road system, yet it was an elaboration and expansion of an earlier system built by the Huari culture of the Middle Horizon. Therefore, a brief description of the major cultural developments in each period follows.

This period begins with the arrival of humans in South America. The original inhabitants of the western hemisphere came from northeastern Russia, following game animals across the *Bering land bridge*. The land bridge existed where the Bering Strait (which separates Alaska from Russia) is today. During the last ice age the sea levels were lower than today, so the straits was actually dry land. After crossing the land bridge, peo-

Preceramic Period (?–1800 B.C.)

ple migrated southward through Canada, North America, and Central America, finally arriving in South America.

The actual date of the arrival of these people in South America is under dispute. A fairly widely accepted date is approximately 13,000 B.C., although some humans might have arrived earlier. At the beginning of this period, people lived in small groups of 25 to 50 individuals. They hunted wild animals and gathered wild plants. *Nomadic*, they moved frequently to find food and shelter. On the basis of cultures today that follow a similar lifestyle, one can say that men probably hunted animals and women gathered plants.

As time went on, however, these groups began to learn more about their environments—whether coastal, highland, or foothills—and to stay in more restricted areas, such as a single valley or river basin. They learned the reproductive cycles of plants and animals, and they ultimately domesticated many species of plants as well as animals such as the llama, alpaca, and guinea pig.

In the highland region the process of domestication began quite early—almost as soon as people arrived, according to remains found in Guitarrero Cave in northern Peru (Lynch 1980). Llamas and alpacas were domesticated by 3000 B.C., with corn, beans, squash, potatoes, and other Andean foods about the same time (Smith 1994/95: 181). On the coast, domesticated foods did not appear until the end of the Preceramic Period; apparently they were introduced from the adjacent highland regions.

Following the domestication of plants and animals, the basic way of life of Andean peoples changed. Villages sprang up as people settled in a single location to be near their fields and pastures. Houses became more permanent and larger, perhaps as a result of the demands of expanding families. In the highlands, following the shift to an agricultural way of life the basic patterns of exploiting the puna, quechua, and yunga zones developed.

Along the coast, people began to use the abundant resources of the Pacific Ocean at a very early date (Sandweiss et al. 1989). Around 2500 B.C., toward the end of the Preceramic Period, there was an increase in the number of settlements located right along the coastline and an associated increase in the use of marine resources. Farming appeared at about the same time, and it is important to note that two of the earliest domesticated plants to appear on the coast were cotton and gourd, both non-edible. These two plants gained importance through their use in the fishing industry. Cotton was used for making fishing lines and nets, and gourds were used as floats for the nets. The fields where these plants were cultivated must have been located in the valley floodplains, which provided the only sources of water for farming.

A new pattern of life may have been established along the coast during this time. Part of the population of a river valley would live along the coast, where they fished, collected shellfish, and gathered seaweed and other marine resources. Another part of the population would live along the rivers, growing gourds, cotton, beans, and squash. The two populations would exchange products. This reflects the first *division of labor* among coastal communities, which was to become much more elaborate in later periods.

One final development of the Preceramic Period was the beginning of large-scale public buildings. Until about 3000 B.C., all constructions in Andean communities were houses or other small structures for ritual or social events. However, between 3000 and 1800 B.C., several very large structures were built at villages both in the highlands and on the coast. These structures are interpreted as having had some kind of ceremonial purposes, rather than being the homes of individuals. They were much larger than the houses of typical families, rising as much as 10 m (33 ft) above the surrounding landscape. Their size reflects a considerable amount of coordinated labor, suggesting not only that these societies were much larger than previous ones but also that leaders were in charge. Thus not only do we see evidence of the first division of labor during this time, but we also infer the emergence of some sort of leaders or rulers.

Several sites along the coast show evidence of these cultural developments, from the area around modern Lima to the vicinity of Trujillo. Two examples are Salinas de Chao, in the Chao valley of northern Peru, and El Paraiso, in the Chillón valley of central Peru. Salinas de Chao was a settlement occupied around a bay that has since dried up. A very large pyramid mound was constructed, which was probably used for ceremonies. A small distance away was an area of housing clustered against a hillside. In front of the houses were two sunken circular pits, which also might have had ceremonial uses. The two different kinds of ceremonial constructions—mound and sunken pit—suggest different kinds of ceremonies, perhaps to distinct gods. Such evidence suggests that even at this early date the inhabitants had a rich religious life.

El Paraiso is located near the mouth of the Chillón River, outside of modern Lima. It is a set of nine large mounds of rubble, resulting from the decomposition of a series of rooms and corridors. Over 100,000 tons of stone were quarried to build the site, indicating that a large amount of labor went into its construction (Moseley 1992: 119). The rooms were built by piling up mesh bags of stone. One complex of rooms has been reconstructed and indicates the enormous size of the original undertaking: the complex is 50 m (165 ft) on a side, and 8 m (26 ft) high. And this is one of the smaller complexes at the site! The size of the site and the amount of labor involved indicate that a large group of people was responsible for its construction, and it is likely that there were individ-

Sunken court, Salinas de Chao, prior to excavation. Note person for scale.
(Courtesy of Sheila and Thomas Pozorski)

uals in charge of the activities. Some have even suggested that people from both farming and fishing communities over a large area contributed labor. The use of mesh bags of stone for construction suggests that there might have been some standard amount of stone that different groups had to contribute to the building activity. This indicates planning, most likely by the authorities in charge. The use of mesh bags for building is known from other contemporary sites such as Aspero, located in the Supe valley north of El Paraiso.

Similar developments were occurring in the highlands to the east of the coast. Temple mounds appeared during this time at the site of Kotosh, near modern Huánuco, and at La Galgada, a remote site on a tributary of the Santa River in northern Peru. These temples are generally smaller than those found along the coast, suggesting that the groups who constructed them were smaller.

An interesting feature common to both Kotosh and La Galgada is the use of small rooms with central *hearths,* or fireplaces, where offerings were burned. The hearths had a ventilation shaft that ran under the floor to the outside of the room. The shaft brought air to the fire, allowing it to burn. This distinctive way of building a ceremonial room suggests that the rituals conducted within them were the same at both sites; hence we can infer that the religious beliefs were the same as well. The common

Reconstructed room complex at El Paraiso, Chillón valley, Peru.

religion is called the *Kotosh Religious Tradition* (Burger and Salazar-Burger 1980). This religious tradition has recently been found at coastal sites, suggesting it may have been even more widespread than previously thought. Indeed, evidence indicates that people were communicating and sharing religious ideas over a large area.

Initial Period (1800–900 B.C.) During the Initial Period, pottery, or baked clay vessels, made their appearance in the area of modern Peru. Along the coast, a much expanded use of domesticated food plants is associated with this development. There was a dramatic shift in the locations of villages, also: many coastal villages were abandoned and new settlements were located much farther inland, away from the ocean. The shift apparently corresponded to an important new development: irrigation. Towns were now located where water could be drawn out of the rivers through small canals to irrigate the fields. This allowed for the expansion of agriculture. Even though many of the earlier fishing villages were abandoned, some continued to be occupied and still exchanged marine products for domesticated ones. However, now agriculture became the most important way of producing food.

It should be noted that the shift to an agricultural way of life supported by marine resource exploitation developed much earlier in coastal Ecuador. There, people had settled down and started farming and using pot-

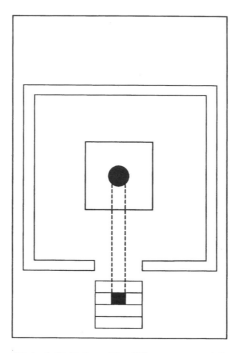

Kotosh Religious Tradition ceremonial
room with subfloor ventilation shaft.
The broken lines represent the
underground shaft leading from a step
outside the room to the base of the
hearth inside.

tery as early as 3000 B.C. in a culture known as Valdivia (Bruhns 1994: 82–
85). Why this way of life developed 1,400 years earlier in Ecuador than
Peru is unknown. Archaeologist Donald Lathrap (1977) thinks Valdivia
culture actually developed in eastern Ecuador in the Amazonian area, and
then spread to the coast as a result of population increase.

Returning to the Peruvian area, Initial Period societies along the coast
became much larger than the preceramic ones that preceded them. Following the opening of the desert to farming by irrigation, populations
apparently increased considerably. Temples and other public buildings
became much larger. True *ceremonial centers* appeared: places to which
people from a wide region came on certain sacred days to worship, but
which had only a small resident population of priests and their helpers.
In turn, the nonresident people provided the labor to build these centers,
under the direction of leaders who may also have been priests.

These societies became more differentiated: the preceramic division of labor expanded. Now people specialized in doing one activity fulltime. In the Casma valley, evidence indicates how complex some societies had become (Pozorski and Pozorski 1987). There, a few small villages are found along the seashore where people caught fish and collected shellfish. This food was apparently taken to authorities in a nearby village, who passed it on to a very large town, Pampa de las Llamas-Moxeque, located in the middle of the valley. Crops grown elsewhere in the valley were also brought to the main town. A very large storage facility was constructed there to house all these products, which in turn were used by the fisherfolk, farmers, and non-food-producing members of the society (Pozorski and Pozorski 1987). Farmers received fish, and fisherfolk received food crops from the storehouse. This evidence argues for the existence of a *government*, a group of people whose fulltime job was to direct what people did and where goods went in society. The government officials lived in the main town and in the small village where the ocean food was brought from the fishing villages.

Small governments appeared all along the coast during the Initial Period, indicating that societies were becoming larger and more specialized. The division of labor now included government officials, not just food producers. Although there is no clear evidence for it, craft activities such as pottery making and stoneworking might also have been fulltime jobs. The rulers of these societies now had much greater responsibilities, such as organizing irrigation, planning construction activities, making sure that everyone received what they needed. The presence at several sites of much larger pyramid mounds than the preceramic ones indicates that religion continued to be important in the people's lives. Whether the religious leaders were also the government leaders is not certain; it is likely they were.

In the highland zones to the east of the coastal societies, similar developments continued as well, yet on a smaller scale. Temple mounds were built, but they were much smaller and seem to reflect a smaller group of people working together. Here, there was no emergence of a government, but simply the continuation of the preceramic way of life with the addition of pottery and new crops.

In other regions of the Andes, developments were not as advanced as along the central and northern coast of Peru. In Ecuador, the way of life begun with the Valdivia culture continued unchanged through this time. Over most of the southern Andes, both in the highlands and along the coast, societies followed a simple farming and fishing or farming and herding way of life. Of note in the Altiplano region was the Chiripa culture, which constructed a small ceremonial center of 16 small buildings arranged around a square courtyard. This is the first example in the southern highlands of the kind of societal differentiation that developed earlier in other parts of Peru.

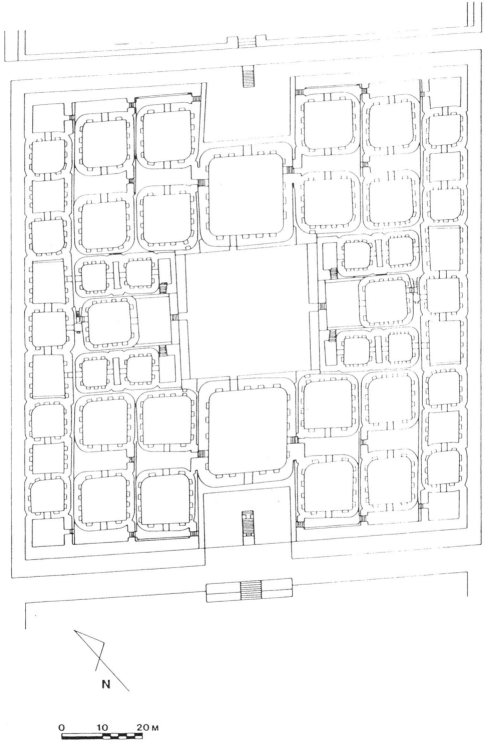

N

0   10   20 м

Huaca A, a large storage facility at the site of Pampa de las Llamas-Moxeque, in the
Casma valley. (Line drawing by Thomas and Sheila Pozorski)

Beginning around 900 B.C., or earlier in some areas, a new and distinctive cultural development appeared in central Peru: Chavin. Apparently it was a kind of religion or cult whose influence spread rapidly across a wide area, from the northern highlands and coast of Peru to the

Early Horizon (900–200 B.C.)

coastal area south of modern Lima (Burger 1988). Chavin is recognized by its highly distinctive art style, which is found on many kinds of objects: stone, bone, shell, clay, and gold. The art style is a reflection of the religious beliefs.

Evidence for the Chavin cult is very unevenly distributed across the central part of Peru. Some coastal societies show abundant evidence in both their pottery and buildings. Along the northern coast the local pottery, called Cupisnique, shows heavy influence in the use of Chavin decorations. The temples there also show influence in the use of large adobe heads and faces with Chavin designs. This suggests the religion was adopted by the rulers, who prominently displayed their devotion on the walls of the temples.

Chavin is named for the site of Chavin de Huántar, which was founded in the central highlands during this time. The town was more than a ceremonial center; it was a true urban center, with a large resident population of farmers, craftspeople, and others (Burger 1992). The site has some of the purest examples of Chavin art and so must have been an important center, although other centers were earlier and larger.

The Early Horizon marks the time in central Andean prehistory when *craft specialization* becomes more evident. Craft specialization involves the making of crafts—pottery, jewelry, clothing, ornaments, stone tools, and the like—by specialists, people who do nothing but make that craft. Although craft specialization may have occurred earlier (as in the Casma valley discussed previously), the quality of the Chavin artifacts argues that it became much more developed during this time. Such a development required even more food to be produced by the farmers and herders, and a larger number of government officials to run the entire economy.

In areas of the southern coast, in the region around Ica, the Early Horizon culture is known as Paracas. This culture was not as large or specialized as the ones farther north; it had no large temples or public buildings. Yet even here we find evidence for the cult in the use of Chavin designs on pottery. This suggests a widespread adoption of the cult by all members of Paracas society, not just the rulers.

In many other areas of the Andes, Chavin influence did not appear; so the societies continued as they had previously. In the southern Andes, around Lake Titicaca, two distinctive cultures—Pucara and Tiahuanaco—emerged during the Early Horizon. Pucara developed at the northwestern end of the lake and shows some similarities to the earlier

Chavin carved stone god, the Lanzón. This figure is over 3 m
(10 ft) high and is located inside the Old Temple at the site of
Chavin de Huántar, Mosna valley, Peru.

Chiripa culture that was located at the southeastern end of the lake. The culture is named for the site of Pucara, a large settlement of houses and other structures that stretched along a river for several kilometers. However, the most important part of the site is a large, stepped building complex that is backed up against a natural hill. At the topmost level is a sunken rectangular area that is very similar to the earlier one at Chiripa. A fine pottery tradition is also present at Pucara, as is a stone scupture tradition. The latter included both animal and human figures, in the round as well as flat relief.

The urban nature of the site of Pucara suggests that its inhabitants were developing distinct occupations, much as societies elsewhere had. The same appears true at Tiahuanaco (located outside of modern La Paz, Bolivia), which was to become a major city during the Early Intermediate Period and Middle Horizon.

This period is marked by the disappearance of Chavin influence. Apparently the religion waned in popularity, and people began worshipping other *deities*, or gods. Societies formerly influenced by the Chavin religion developed their own distinctive art styles. Coastal societies continued to increase in population, leading to more job specialization and even larger governments. Warfare began to play a much greater role as societies became larger. For the first time, a few cultures began to dominate several valleys. In the highlands, militarism appears to have increased as well, although no culture dominated an area larger than a single river valley.

Early Intermediate Period (200 B.C.–A.D. 600)

The most famous Early Intermediate Period culture was the Moche, or Mochica, of the northern coast of Peru. This society conquered areas to the north and south of its home valley of Moche. We know a considerable amount about the Moche because of their beautifully made ceramics decorated with scenes from their lifestyles. According to Christopher Donnan, one of the foremost authorities on the Moche, they were ruled by warrior priests who engaged in ritual drinking of war captives' blood (Donnan 1988, 1990). Below these rulers were other political and religious individuals who played prominent roles in Moche society. The Moche had whole groups of craftspeople who made exquisite artifacts of gold, silver, copper, shell, and precious stones. At the bottom of the social ladder were farmers and fisherfolk.

The Moche was one of the first societies to bury important individuals in pyramid mounds. In fact, one of the most significant archaeological discoveries of this century was the undisturbed tomb of a Moche lord found at Sipán, in the Lambayeque valley on the northern coast (Alva 1988, 1990). This tomb contained a fabulous collection of gold and silver objects, thousands of shell beads, feather plumes, and other precious stones, all preserved by the dry environment. Most im-

Moche vessel, showing a warrior figure in full battle dress. Vessel from collection in the Phoebe A. Hearst Museum of Anthropology, University of California, Berkeley. (Courtesy of Donald Proulx)

portant, however, the discovery showed for the first time that the figures on Moche pottery were not mythical but real, and that the scenes were from real life, not fantastic depictions of gods. From the pottery, the tombs at Sipán, and other remains, it is evident that the Moche had a powerful and highly developed society, much more so than any previous societies.

In other areas of the coast, societies did not reach the level of Moche political development but still were larger and more differentiated than previous ones. The Nasca culture of the southern coastal region developed out of the earlier Paracas culture. This society is known for its beautiful multicolored pottery, its textiles, and its curious tradition of making *geoglyphs,* lines and figures scraped into the surface of the ground. The latter are often referred to as Nazca Lines. (The spelling "Nazca" is used for the geographical location; "Nasca" refers to the ancient culture that lived in the Nazca region.)

The geoglyphs include lines many kilometers long, oblong geometric shapes, and animal figures. There are many explanations for why they were made, ranging from sacred spaces to astronomical markers—even landing fields for aliens from outer space! In fact, it is difficult to say

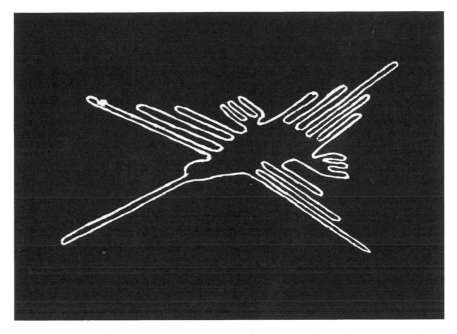

Nasca geoglyph of a hummingbird. The figure was formed by clearing the
dark desert surface away to expose the lighter soil.

exactly what they meant to the people who made them. Helaine Silverman (1990), an authority on Nasca culture, suggests they were probably
sacred symbols for local groups of related people, constructed as part of
rituals to their gods. She mentions that many of the lines seem to lead
to Cahuachi, the largest and most complex Nasca settlement. The settlement consisted of over 40 mounds of varying sizes and shapes, but few
houses. Whereas some scholars suggest Cahuachi was the political capital of the Nasca culture, Silverman argues it was more of a ceremonial
center to which Nascans came during certain times of the year to participate in rituals.

Other than Cahuachi, there are relatively few large Nasca towns. The
population seems to have been dispersed across the landscape in small
villages of the middle regions of the Ica and Nazca river drainages. A
unique feature of Nasca agriculture was the use of tunnels bored into
hillsides to reach underground streams for irrigating their fields (Schreiber 1995).

In the highland regions the Early Intermediate Period societies also

Recuay stone sculptures. The lintel in the foreground shows feline and human
figures. Note the figure in the background.

became more differentiated, although they did not reach the levels of
complexity seen in the Moche. A little-known but interesting culture
known as Recuay existed in the Callejón de Huaylas, due east of the
Casma valley during this time. Almost all that is known of this culture
comes from its exquisite pottery and stone sculptures. The pottery is of
an unusual white clay known as *kaolin.* Scenes on Recuay pottery depict
warriors, women, serpents, cat-like figures, and condors, all in a highly
repetitive style. The sculptures are squat figures of both men and women,
the former generally armed with clubs and shields. Stone heads that
were fastened to buildings are also found. These heads are reminiscent
of the stone sculpture of nearby Chavin de Huántar and likely developed
from that tradition.

In the Lake Titicaca region the Tiahuanaco culture, which had its beginnings in the Early Horizon, reached the height of its development.
The capital of this culture was the city of Tiahuanaco, a large urban
center with a ceremonial section in the middle that consisted of several
large enclosed courtyard areas and a stone-faced mound. Around this
section was a much larger area where lower-level members of society
probably lived and worked (Kolata 1983: 258). In the general area around
Tiahuanaco were other political centers of lesser importance, as well as
farming villages.

Tiahuanaco is located on the Altiplano, virtually all of which lies in

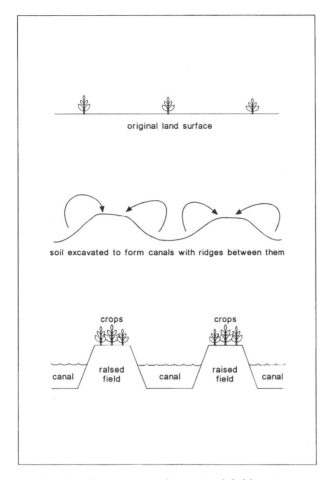

original land surface

soil excavated to form canals with ridges between them

crops   crops

canal / raised field   canal   raised field \ canal

Construction sequence for a raised field system.

the puna zone. Because of the altitude, agriculture is exceedingly difficult and virtually all that grows are potatoes and other hardy plants of this zone. In addition, near Lake Titicaca the ground is flat and the water table is high, which makes farming difficult. The Tiahuanaco people used an ingenious method of *raised fields* for dealing with these problems. A raised field is built by digging a trench and piling the earth up to form a raised area above the trench. By building several of these together and connecting the ditches, one gets a system of low areas, the ditches, which fill up with water, and high areas, the fields, where crops can be planted. The advantages of raised fields are that they (1) allow cold night air to run off the fields into the ditches, thus reducing frost damage, and (2) provide better drainage for the plants. Experiments done with modern fields constructed in the ancient manner indicate that they are much more productive than cultivation without raised fields (Erickson 1988).

The rulers of Tiahuanaco developed a vast system of raised fields to increase the yields of crops, both to feed their population and for trade. Because many important crops—such as corn, beans, squash, and fruits—cannot be grown on the Altiplano, they must be obtained from regions lower down. One of the main reasons for the growth of Tiahuanaco is thought to be the trade that developed between it and towns and villages at lower altitudes. Tiahuanaco pottery is found widely at settlements all over the Southern Andes, from northwest Argentina and northern Chile to southern Peru. Tiahuanaco also founded colonies in these regions, but they are distinct from the settlements of local groups.

Trade was conducted by llama caravan. The Altiplano area is excellent for herding, because there are vast expanses of grasslands. Llamas were raised for carrying the highland products to lower regions in exchange for the crops of those areas. Alpacas were bred for their wool, which was no doubt one of the exports from this region and was used as well for making warm clothing for the local people.

There is little evidence that the spread of Tiahuanaco influence outside the Altiplano was by conquest, because relatively few settlements in other areas during this time were fortified. It is more likely that its influence was spread by trading contacts. In addition, the religious beliefs of Tiahuanaco may have spread as a byproduct of the economic activities: individuals from the more powerful Altiplano center came to small villages and towns, and because of their importance and high status the local people tried to imitate them, including converting to their religion. Thus Tiahuanaco pottery and religious images spread across a wide area without the need of a strong army.

Middle Horizon (A.D. 600–1000) The Middle Horizon is the second period during which large areas were integrated by a cultural force. In this case it was the expansion of two powerful societies: one that spread through economic activities, the other through militaristic means. The first, Tiahuanaco, has already been discussed. Its influence continued to expand during this period, although it fell into decline toward the end. The other culture, Huari, was located in the central Peruvian highlands near the modern city of Ayacucho. It apparently began to develop at the beginning of the Middle Horizon, then expanded and collapsed, all before A.D. 1000.

One of the most interesting aspects of these two cultures is the similarity in the decorations on their pottery. Both used essentially the same stylized figures: a human with outstretched arms holding a staff in each arm, and other figures that look like kneeling or running angels. Some differences do exist, such as the presence of a female figure on Huari

Staff God, from Gateway of the Sun, Tiahuanaco, Bolivia. (Courtesy of Lars Fogelin)

pottery (Bruhns 1994: 247). Assuming that the figures are associated with the religious beliefs of these people, it can be assumed that they shared similar, although not identical, beliefs.

However, the shared beliefs are virtually the only things the two cultures had in common. As mentioned, Tiahuanaco appears to have spread its influence through economic and religious means. In contrast, Huari apparently increased its influence by military means (Isbell and McEwan 1993; Schreiber 1992). Some archaeologists believe the Huari influence, like Tiahuanaco's, was economic (Moseley 1992). The capital of this culture was the site of Huari, located near Ayacucho in the highlands east of modern-day Lima. Like Tiahuanaco, the city was very large and divided into distinct sections. Unlike Tiahuanaco, most of the major buildings do not appear to have been ceremonial in nature; rather, they may have served as centers of craft production and storage. Farming was done outside the city.

In contrast to the Altiplano, the major limitation to agriculture in this area—and in fact in many highland valleys—was the shortage of flat land for fields and the uncertainties in yearly rainfall. Huari people re-

Terracing in the Colca valley, Peru. These were probably built during the
Middle Horizon. They are no longer in use.

duced these dangers by building *terraces*, which were made by constructing a stone wall and filling in the area behind and uphill from it
with soil. Terraces provide flat areas for planting; they were generally
constructed one above another, like stairs going up the side of mountain. In addition, irrigation canals were dug to bring water to the terraces. One of the important developments during the Middle Horizon
all over the area of Huari influence was the increase in the number of
terraces. This suggests it was the Huari who introduced the technology
to other people.

Huari influence is also seen in the appearance of its typical pottery in
areas distant from Ayacucho and in the highly distinctive building style
of its political centers (Isbell 1993). The Huari established control over
conquered areas by building large centers that served as warehouses and
residences for the rulers of these regions. The centers are found as far
north as the Cajamarca region in the northern Peruvian highlands. To
the south, the Huari empire stopped where Tiahuanaco's began, in

southern Peru. Apparently the two empires were unfriendly, although just how much conflict there was between them is not certain.

Archaeologists do not agree on what sort of relationship existed between Tiahuanaco and Huari. Some feel that because Tiahuanaco developed earlier, it must have been influential in the growth and expansion of Huari. Others feel that the two cultures were so different that they must have developed independently of one another. It remains to be determined why they shared religious beliefs yet were so different otherwise.

In the northern Andes, outside the sphere of Huari influence, some societies continued to grow in size and political complexity while others remained small and simple. A new and powerful society, Sicán, emerged on the northern coast of Peru following the decline of the Moche. This culture continued some of the traditions of the Moche: they buried their kings with an immense wealth of gold, silver, copper, and bronze objects, exquisite pottery, wooden implements, exotic seashells, and offerings of human sacrifices. They expanded contacts with cultures to the north in Ecuador, and trade goods of each society have been found in the other's towns (Bruhns 1994: 294–297).

This was again a time of regional development, as the integrating influences of Huari and Tiahuanaco broke down. Local cultures created their own ways of doing things, reflected by the appearance of new decorative techniques, especially on pottery. Populations continued to grow, however; and this period was **Late Intermediate Period (A.D. 1000–1438)** marked by an increase in conflicts, both within local cultures and between them. Many settlements moved to locations that could be defended, especially ridgetops. Walls and other defensive structures became more commonplace. Even the early Spanish writers, some of whom asked native people what life was like prior to the Inca conquests, noted that these peoples talked about the abundant warfare among their pre-Inca ancestors.

Political organization over the area that was to become Tahuantinsuyu was highly varied. Some societies still functioned at a relatively simple farming level, whereas others had complex governments, craft specialization, and a developed ruling class. Probably the most complex society was the Chimu of the northern coast of Peru. This group expanded out of the Moche valley sometime after A.D. 1000 and conquered all the valleys from Lambayeque to the area around modern Lima. They were entirely a coastal culture, however, never conquering groups in the adjacent highlands.

The Chimu capital was a city called Chan Chan, located on the Pacific Ocean outside the modern city of Trujillo. This city, built entirely of mud bricks, was over 6 km² (2.2 mi²) in size. The focus of the city was ten

Outside wall of a ciudadela at Chan Chan, Moche valley, Peru.

huge walled compounds, called *ciudadelas*, which were combination warehouses, administrative centers, royal residences, and burial places of the kings (Day 1982). The outside walls of the ciudadelas were often more than 10 m high, emphasizing the private nature of the activities that went on within them. The shape and layout of the ciudadelas may have been influenced by the Huari administrative centers, although the Huari empire never extended to the northern coast.

Scattered around the ciudadelas were smaller compounds that served as residences and places of work for lower-level political leaders. There were also numerous smaller buildings that were the homes and workshops of craftspeople. The craftspeople were dependent on the small compounds for food and water, and the goods they manufactured were distributed to the small compounds and ciudadelas. Apparently all the residents of Chan Chan were nonfood producers. The farmers lived in separate settlements among the fields in the Moche valley and brought their products into the city, either to the ciudadelas or to the small compounds, from which the products were distributed to the craftspeople (Klymyshyn 1982; Topic 1982).

Atahuallpa meets Pizarro near Cajamarca.

The Chimu established administrative centers in other valleys to collect food and for the manufacture of crafts, such as weaving. The relationship of these centers to Chan Chan is not clearly understood. The pottery produced at Chimu settlements was a distinctive black color and was mass-produced in molds. Other crafts indicate a high level of quality and skill. It is known from Spanish accounts that the best craftspeople were taken from Chan Chan to the Inca capital of Cuzco after the Chimu were conquered.

In addition to the Chimu, a series of other multivalley political groups existed down the Peruvian coast and in the highlands from Ecuador to Bolivia. Most lived in large towns, many of which were fortified to some extent. One of these small cultures was the Inca, located in the southern highlands of Peru. During the Late Intermediate Period they began a series of small-scale conquests of the groups living in areas adjacent to their capital of Cuzco. These groups later became some of the Incas' most loyal allies and were given the honorary title of "Inca-by-privilege."

Late Horizon
(A.D. 1438–1532)

This period begins in A.D. 1438, when the Incas defeated the Chanca and when Pachacuti became the ninth king. The Late Horizon was the time of the Inca expansion under Pachacuti, Topa Inca, and Huayna Capac, when Inca settlements and artifacts began to appear all over the Andes. In A.D. 1527, Huayna Capac died suddenly—possibly from smallpox that spread into South America from Central America, where it had been introduced by the Spanish explorers. Huayna Capac's heir also died, without naming an heir to replace him. Another of Huayna Capac's sons, Huascar, who lived in Cuzco, was then proclaimed king. However, another son, Atahuallpa, who had lived with Huayna Capac in Quito, claimed that he had been given the northern provinces to rule. The armies of each brother went to war, with Atahuallpa's consistently victorious over Huascar's. After the final battle outside Cuzco, all the nobles who had been loyal to Huascar were hunted down and put to death, thereby removing all threats to Atahuallpa's claims to the throne. Atahuallpa heard the news of the Spaniards' arrival in northern Peru about the same time he heard the news of his army's final triumph over Huascar.

The Spanish explorer Pizarro landed on the northern coast of Peru in A.D. 1532. Atahuallpa was traveling south to Cuzco, to be invested as Inca king. Through interpreters Atahuallpa agreed to meet the Spaniards near the northern city of Cajamarca. The Spaniards staged a surprise attack when his party entered the meeting area, and he was captured. They held him for ransom, which was said to be a room half-filled with gold and silver. The Incas stripped many of their buildings in Cuzco of these metals to ransom their king, but to no avail. Pizarro ordered Atahuallpa strangled, after which the Spaniards proceeded to Cuzco, set up a puppet ruler as king, and began the dismantling of the empire.

2

Politics and Society

The Incas built their empire in less than a century. This in itself was an extraordinary achievement, but other empires have expanded as rapidly or even more so. For example, Alexander the Great's conquests of the Middle East occurred in less than 30 years. Conquering people is a relatively straightforward thing to do; all one needs is many well-armed soldiers and effective military leaders. However, to integrate conquered peoples into a single empire that functions as a unit with central control is much more difficult. This is especially so when the conquered societies are spread out over a broad area of very rugged terrain, such as the Andes mountains. Perhaps the greatest achievement of the Incas is that they appear to have successfully organized all the groups they conquered into an empire that did function as a unit. This is not to say the empire ran smoothly; quite to the contrary, the history of the Inca empire is one of rebellions and conflict. It is also apparent that the Incas did not use a single policy of incorporation for every conquered group; rather, they tailored their policies to the particular circumstances of each group (Malpass 1993a).

One of the reasons for the Incas' success was their use of the existing political and social structures of conquered people for ruling them. Instead of trying to change the people's lives, they tried to maintain continuity so the subjects' lives were disrupted as little as possible. The Incas saw their relationship to conquered peoples as one of *institutionalized reciprocity* (Morris 1978). This means that the Incas expected the conquered people to work for them, but in return they provided them with services and goods, food and clothing, beer, coca, and even entertainment. They assigned conquered leaders positions of authority in the government, gave them high-status gifts, and honored their religious beliefs and practices. In return the Incas expected the conquered people to work hard for them, to produce, among other things, food, cloth, pottery, buildings, and other large and small items; and to be obedient and loyal subjects. How the Incas organized their empire to do this is the topic of this chapter.

Warfare in the Andes was fought with
spears, clubs, slings, and shields.

MILITARY ORGANIZATION AND WARFARE

Certainly one of the key reasons for the Incas' success in building their empire was their military organization. Their superior army, leaders, equipment, and tactics helped them to defeat their enemies. The highly disciplined army mainly comprised people recruited from already-conquered groups. Warfare in the Andes was basically hand-to-hand combat with clubs and spears, and the Inca army was very well armed by Andean standards. Bows and arrows were not a highland weapon, although the Incas employed tropical forest groups who did use them. A more common weapon that could be used from a distance was the sling. Moreover *bolas*, a group of leather straps tied together with rocks at their ends, were used for bringing enemies down: a warrior would throw his bola around the enemy's legs. Defensive weapons included shields and cotton armor (Rowe 1946: 274–279).

One of the most important considerations of warfare is providing food and supplies for the soldiers. This was as true for the Incas as it is today. Given how rapidly the Inca armies expanded the empire, the problem of providing food to them as they advanced up and down the spine of the Andes must have been considerable. One of the keys to this success was the Inca road system (see the section below on Engineering and Architecture). The Incas constructed roads to connect the different parts of their empire, and along the roads they placed major Inca cities where food and clothing were stored.

The Incas did not always have to rely on force to subdue other groups. Spanish writers reported that the Incas sent representatives in an effort to reach terms of submission without warfare, and apparently they were successful in many instances (Rowe 1946: 281). Other groups, however, chose either to fight or to flee. One group burned their fields and villages so the Incas would not be able to use their food or houses.

If a group fought the Incas it usually was defeated, with many men killed in battle. The group would then have to submit to the Incas demands. If the group chose to run away, it was forced to live in another region away from where it and its ancestors had always lived. Because there were few unpopulated areas, a group that fled the Incas probably had to stay with neighbors or allies in more distant areas. This might simply have postponed its conquest, if the Incas then attacked the lands where it had moved. Finally, if the people submitted without a fight, no one was killed but they had to meet the tribute demands of the Incas.

The Incas' terms of conquest were relatively simple, but severe. Ownership of the lands of conquered people was claimed by the Inca king, although the people were allowed to use it. The land was divided into three parts: one for the Inca state, one for the Inca religion, and one for the conquered people's use. Local leaders were given positions in the Inca bureaucracy and left to rule as before. However, their sons were taken to Cuzco and trained in Inca policies. When the old leader died his son would replace him, bringing to the job his new knowledge and the Inca point of view. Finally, the Incas allowed conquered people to continue worshipping their own gods, but they had to acknowledge the superiority of the Inca gods. The Incas bestowed honor on the sacred objects of conquered people by setting up a shrine for them in Cuzco. Although this seems generous and noble, the Incas had a political reason for doing it: the objects were held hostage with the threat if the people rebelled, the Incas might damage or destroy them.

GOVERNMENT

The Four Quarters   The second key to the Incas' success in forming a unified empire was their organization of conquered peoples. Pachacuti, the ninth king, is credited with setting up the empire and making it run effectively, although it is possible that the process began earlier (Bauer 1992). The empire was divided into four *suyus*, or divisions: Chinchaysuyu (north), Collasuyu (south), Antisuyu (east), and Cuntisuyu (west), which radiated from the capital city of Cuzco. The suyus were not equal in size; the north and south divisions were large, and the east and west quarters were small (see Map in Introduction).

Each quarter was made up of several *provinces*. A province usually corresponded to the area occupied by a conquered people. If the conquered group was small, it might be added to other small ones to make a single province. If a conquered group was large, like the Chimu, it might be divided into more than one province. The ideal was to have approximately 20,000 households in a province. Households were the basic unit in most Andean societies, and they generally corresponded to a family. However, unlike the concept of family in U.S. society (a mother and father and their children), Andean families might also include grandparents, grandchildren, aunts, or uncles.

Administration   The Inca empire was administered by a well-developed bureaucracy that collected tribute and distributed it. At the top was the king, who was the ultimate authority on all matters. Below the king were four officials, called *apos*, each in charge of one of the quarters. These officials were close advisors of the king and probably relatives as well. Each province had a governor who was responsible for its affairs. There were more than 80 provinces in the Inca empire, so this added 80 or more individuals to the bureaucracy. Each governor was under the orders of the apo of the quarter in which his province lay.

The 20,000-household province was set up so it could be most effectively ruled. The system was *hierarchical* in that officials lower down were responsible to ones higher up and it was based on a decimal system of counting, like that of most modern countries today. Below each provincial governor were two government officials called *curacas*, who were in charge of 10,000 households each. The curacas were each in charge of two curacas of 5,000 households. The curacas in turn directed the activities of five curacas who managed 1,000 households each. The lowest-level administrators were two curacas who had responsibility for 500 households and five curacas who handled 100 households each.

What did all the curacas do? Their chief responsibility was to make sure the proper number of people showed up to work for the Incas, and to distribute the workload among the households for which each was responsible. It was also the curaca's duty to ensure the correct amount of tribute was produced and transported to the nearest Inca center, and to allocate to each household adequate land to support itself. If a curaca did a good job, he was rewarded by his superiors; if not, he was punished. Punishments ranged from public rebuke to death, depending on whether the individual was merely being lazy or actually dishonest.

Inca law applied to many activities such as tribal rights, division of land, policy of rotation for work, and even support of the el-   **Law** derly and disabled (Kendall 1973: 59). Inca law was quite severe, laying out strict punishments for many offenses. The higher the status of the individual, the more severe the punishment for a crime. For example, adultery among commoners was punishable by torture; but if the woman was a noble, both parties were executed. Crimes against the government were treated with special severity. Stealing from the fields of the state was punishable by death. If a curaca put a person to death without permission of his superior, a stone was dropped on his back from a height of three feet. If he did it again, he was killed. Treason was punished by imprisoning the person in an underground prison in Cuzco that was filled with snakes and dangerous animals. The person rarely survived the imprisonment (Rowe 1946: 271).

The judicial system was based on the administrative one, with the appropriate curaca presiding over the proceedings. For example, if a case involved grievances of one individual against another but both were within the same unit of 100 households, then the curaca of that unit officiated. However, if the case was against an individual from another unit of 100, then the curaca of 500 who was in charge of both would be the official. Crimes punishable by death, such as those mentioned above, were taken to the provincial governor or king (Rowe 1946: 271).

LANGUAGE

The language spoken by the Incas is called Quechua. This language was originally spoken by several distinct ethnic groups who lived in the same area of the Andes as the Incas. The name actually comes from an ethnic group called the Quechua who lived to the north of the Incas but who were absorbed into the empire very early. One major problem that the Incas faced in trying to incorporate many conquered people into their empire was the language barrier. Probably dozens of different languages were spoken by people conquered by the Incas, and little is known about how communication was achieved between the Incas and them. The Incas required conquered leaders to learn Quechua, and their sons were taken to Cuzco for instruction that must have included language. How people learned Quechua in the conquered areas is unknown, but it might have been through contact with Inca officials—either in their home villages or at the administrative centers where they worked. After the Spaniards arrived they found it convenient to continue using Quechua, because it was the most widely understood language in use. As a result, Quechua is still spoken by millions of people in areas from Ecuador to Chile, and it is the official second language of Peru.

The Incas had no written language. As a result, all that is known about Inca Quechua comes from the early Spanish writers, none of whom used any fixed rules concerning how the language should be written. Thus it is not uncommon to see different spellings for the same word, for example *Quichua* for *Quechua*. In addition, the Spanish writers often substituted letters that were familiar from their own language. Thus *b* is often substituted for *p*, *g* for *k*, and *gu* or *hu* for *w*. For example, instead of the Quechua *pampa* or *waka*, there is *bamba* and *huaca*.

SOCIAL ORGANIZATION

Kin Groups
All societies have rules or patterns of behavior that govern people's actions. Sometimes these are made official as laws; more often they are simply accepted behaviors by which the members of the society live. *Social organization* refers to the patterns of behavior governing the interactions between individuals, including who one can marry, where newlyweds will live, how the family is defined, what behavior is appropriate to one's in-laws, and so on. The basic unit of Inca social organization was the household. Households were grouped into *ayllus*, groups of related individuals and families who exchanged labor and cooperated in subsistence and ritual activities. Generally ayllus had some kind of leaders, although their authority was limited. Ayllus had territories within which they were located, but the boundaries were not clearly delineated. One of the main functions of the ayllu was to organize labor for activities related to agriculture, such as clearing and preparing fields, irrigation canals, and pastureland. Another function was to regulate marriage, by defining who was an appropriate partner. Ayllu members generally married within the ayllu. Finally, ayllus were important as foci of ritual activities, integrating the members through shared beliefs and ceremonies.

Members of an ayllu were required to marry within their
own ayllu. Although Rowe (1946: 254) states that descent was   **Marriage**
traced on the father's side of the family, Silverblatt (1987: 6–   **Patterns**
7) and others cite Spanish sources as indicating that women,
too, held control over land and herds. Silverblatt argues that there were
dual patterns of inheritance, some through the male line, others through
the female line.

Apparently most of the Incas were monogamous, having only one
spouse. However, any man could have more than one wife if he had
sufficient wealth to support them. The king was allowed as many wives
as he wanted. But to keep the blood line of the king pure, he was required to have an official wife, the *coya*, who was supposed to be his full
sister. It was from the children of this couple that the heir to the throne
was picked by the reigning king (Rowe 1946: 257).

Ayllus were not unique to the Incas; they were widespread over the
Andes. But the Incas gave the ayllus unique political purposes, by group-
ing them together into decimal units of households for taxation purposes.

This brings up an important aspect of the term *Inca*. One must be
careful how the term is used. In different contexts it can refer to a people,
an empire, or even a single person—the Inca king. The term as it is used
by experts refers only to the small ethnic group that originally lived in
the area around Cuzco. All others were not originally Incas; we may
refer to them as Inca subjects, but not as Incas (Moseley 1992: 9).

To be an Inca was to have certain privileges not allowed to others: to
wear a particular kind of headband and to wear earplugs that were so
large that they stretched out the earlobe. This caused the Incas to be
given the Spanish nickname *orejones*, or "big ears" (Rowe 1946: 261). Not
to be an Inca was to be subject to the orders of the reigning Inca king,
who claimed ownership of your land and rights to your labor. Thus the
differences between Inca and Inca subject were great. For this reason, it
is necessary to contrast the Incas and Inca subjects with respect to daily
life in the empire.

The social organization of the Incas was based on the relative close-
ness of one's family to the Inca king (Bauer 1992: Ch. 2). There were
three categories of importance: the Incas of royal blood, the non-royal
Incas of Cuzco, and the Incas-by-privilege. The Incas of royal blood
were directly related to the Inca kings and were therefore ultimately
related to the founding ancestor of all Incas, Manco Capac. The Incas
had an interesting system of passing on power and authority. As will
be discussed in more detail in Chapter 5, they practiced a form of ancestor worship whereby a king, although dead, was still considered to
be an important member of society. Therefore his responsibilities continued in death as they did in life, including taking care of his family.

As a king had many wives and children, this required large quantities of food and goods. When a king died, his royal ayllu became a corporate group, called a *panaca*, that continued to use his wealth to feed its members. The new king then started a new ayllu. There were eleven royal ayllus at the time of the European invasion, corresponding to the first eleven kings; Huascar and Atahuallpa did not have time to form their own.

Thus a new king had to find a source of wealth for himself and his ayllu members. This involved using the power and authority of the office of king to obtain land, goods, and services. Some experts think this may be why the Incas began their wars of conquest: the new kings had to conquer additional lands to gain wealth for themselves, because all the lands around Cuzco had been taken by earlier kings (Conrad and Demarest 1984).

In addition to the royal ayllus, there were ten ayllus of non-royal Incas. These were Inca people who were not related to the kings but lived in or near Cuzco. In the Inca origin myth, these people descended from the groups recruited by the eight original Incas who emerged from the cave at Pacariqtambo. Their ayllus were somewhat lower in status and were lumped into one of two *moieties* (i.e., divisions of a society into two parts). For the Inca, there was an Upper (Hanansaya) and Lower (Hurinsaya) moiety. These moieties chiefly functioned to divide ritual activities among the ayllus of each. Panacas, too, were divided into the two moieties. The Incas imposed the moiety system on their subjects, although it is possible that a similar division may have been present prior to the Inca conquests.

Social Hierarchy   There were several kinds of citizens in the Inca empire. The social status of each was defined by kinship and occupation rather than income (see Table below). The highest-status members of the empire were the Incas, made up of members of the royal and non-royal ayllus, who are often called "Inca-by-blood" in the literature. They were descended from the original Incas who settled in Cuzco. The Inca status also included another, larger group called "Inca-by-privilege." These were groups who also spoke Quechua that lived near the valley of Cuzco (Bauer 1992; Rowe 1946: 261). The Incas-by-privilege were especially important during the period of imperial expansion. The ruling elite used the Incas-by-privilege as the empire's administrators and colonists. Because the empire expanded so rapidly, there were apparently not enough members of the Inca-by-blood ayllus to fill all the government posts. It was necessary to extend the concept of nobility (i.e., "being Inca") to another group so there would be enough Inca-class people to fill the posts. The Inca-by-privilege groups were also used extensively as colonists, being extremely loyal to the empire and knowledgeable about its policies.

Inca Social Hierarchy

Inca: Inca-by-blood

                   11 royal panacas

                   10 non-royal ayllus

                   Inca-by-privilege

Curaca: curacas (lower nobility)

Laborer class: conquered people

Curacas. Another social status in Inca society was that of curaca, or lower nobility. This was the group of government officials who were part of the administrative hierarchy—the curacas of 5,000 or 100 taxpayers, for example, plus their descendants. These people were either leaders of conquered groups or other individuals with administrative capabilities (Rowe 1946: 261).

Labor class. Although it is unmentioned by Spanish chroniclers of the conquest, there must also have been another status in the empire: the conquered people who were not leaders, hence not incorporated as curacas. This class carried out the day-to-day activities that allowed the empire to function. They provided food and labor for the construction of the cities and monuments for which the Incas are famous.

Mitimas. A special status in the Inca empire were the *mitimas.* Mitima were people living away from their place of birth, people who had been moved to another area. There were two kinds of mitima, defined by their role in the empire. One kind allowed the Incas to gain access to certain zones. For example, if all of a conquered people were living in the puna zone, the Inca might move mitimas into the quechua zone of that area to increase the amount of crops grown there (see Chapter 1). As corn was the most important crop to the Incas, very often the Incas moved mitimas into the quechua zones to increase its production there.

The second kind of mitima was political, it afforded control over rebellious people. Groups who were difficult to conquer, or who rebelled after their initial conquest, might be moved from their native homeland to another part of the empire. Typically they were moved into an area among more loyal groups, so they would be less likely to cause additional problems (Rowe 1946: 269). Loyal mitimas, often Inca-by-privilege, would then be moved into the vacated lands to continue producing food there. This must have been a very effective means of control: imagine how psychologically devastating it would be to be removed from the lands where your ancestors had lived to a new region that was totally foreign, and to be forced to live among people whom you neither knew nor trusted.

**From
Kinship
to Empire**

It is important to note that one of the keys to the Incas' success in forging an empire from conquered peoples was the way they manipulated social organization for political purposes. When a group was conquered, its ayllus were grouped into two administrative units of 10,000 households each; these were called *sayas,* and each had an official (a curaca) in charge of it. This division of a conquered people into two equal units corresponded to the Inca moiety system, and each saya was called by the Inca moiety terms, Hanansaya and Hurinsaya. The ayllus were then organized into the administrative units of 5,000, 1,000, 500, and 100 households. Even though most administrative ayllus organized by the Incas were essentially the same as the pre-Inca social ones, the Incas did manipulate the latter to conform to their decimal administrative ones. If there were too few ayllus to make two saya, additional ones from elsewhere would be included. If there were too many, they could be divided into additional units (Rowe 1946: 263). This policy had the effect of making the ayllu less kinship-based and more residence-based. It no doubt weakened the ties binding the members of the ayllus and made them easier to control.

The Incas assimilated the local leaders of conquered people into the Inca administrative bureaucracy by making them curacas. The Incas also made the curaca positions hereditary, to provide stability in the governance of the empire. Sons of curacas were taken to Cuzco and trained, then returned to rule when their fathers died.

At what level the conquered leaders were assigned posts depended on the size of the group they originally controlled. If an ethnic group made up of 100 households conquered by the Incas was ruled by a single leader, he would be made a curaca of 100 households. If the group had 500 households, the leader would become a curaca of 500 households.

It is not certain what happened if a group had, for example, 700 households. Presumably the conquered leader would become a curaca of 500 households, and the remaining 200 would be lumped with 300 others under another curaca of 500 households. The other curaca might be either another member of the conquered group or an outsider, the conquered leader of the group of 300 that was lumped together with the remaining 200 households. One way by which odd numbers of households could be rounded off was through the system of mitima.

In summary, the Incas organized local social units into administrative ones and thereby made control and taxation more efficient. If people were rebellious, they were moved to new areas and loyal subjects replaced them so food productivity would not drop. Quechua was made the official language of the empire. But a conquered group's basic way of life was little changed: they continued to worship their own gods, be ruled by their own leaders, and live the same agricultural way of life they always had. However, much greater amounts of work were required of them.

ECONOMY

Economy refers to the management of a society's resources, including the way people produce and distribute food, raw materials, and manufactured goods. It is important to note that the Inca economy was not based on money. There was no common standard of value, such as the dollar in U.S. society today. Goods were bartered between individuals,

Andean agriculture: harvesting corn.

who negotiated the relative worth of each object. Items exchanged included surplus food and manufactured items—for example, tools, pottery, or objects of personal adornment such as jewelry. Because the Incas

SESTA CALLE
CORO·TASQVE

A 12-year-old Andean boy herding llamas,
spinning wool, and carrying wood.

controlled trade between regions, everything exchanged was strictly local (Rowe 1946: 270). Therefore the range of goods exchanged was relatively restricted.

Land was not owned by individuals. It belonged to a person's ayllu; one had the right to use the land but not to sell it. However, by official decree the Inca king owned all the land of the empire and gave each ayllu the use of its land. The only things a person actually owned were the personal objects she or he obtained, either by gifts or barter.

Agriculture. For the Incas, the main means of subsistence was agriculture, the sowing and reaping of domesticated plants and the breeding of domesticated animals. The Andes are one of the several places in the world where many plants and animals were originally domesticated as people learned their cycles of reproduction. An entire range of plants was grown by Andean

Subsistence Activities

Planting potatoes, using a footplow clod-
breaker.

people in the different environmental zones (see Chapter 1). The most important crop grown was corn, also known as *maize*. Corn beer, called *chicha*, was consumed in large quantities as a dietary drink and during important ceremonies.

A wide variety of other crops was also grown, including potatoes, *quinoa* (a mid-altitude grain with a high protein content), *oca* and *ullucu* (two high-altitude tubers, similar in use to potatoes but different in flavor and shape), many different kinds of beans and squash, sweet potatoes, *manioc* and *yuca* (both starchy, low-altitude tubers), tomatoes, chili peppers, avocadoes, and peanuts (Rowe 1946: 210). Other non-edible plants were also grown, such as coca (chewed with lime to withstand cold and fatigue), cotton, and gourds. The two main domesticated animals were llamas and alpacas; the former was used as a pack animal, and the latter's soft wool was used for clothing. Ducks and guinea pigs were raised for food as well.

As discussed in Chapter 1, these plants and animals were exploited in different combinations in different environmental zones. The Incas used these zones very effectively, in terms of both the crops grown and the use of people to grow them. Farming implements were very simple: a footplow, hoe, and clod-breaker were used for preparing fields for planting. The footplow turned up large chunks of earth, which were then crushed with the clod-breaker, a club-like tool. The hoe, whose blade came straight out from the handle rather than at a 90-degree angle (like that of modern hoes), was used for weeding and breaking up clods as well (Rowe 1946: 211). In the absence of draft animals, these were the only tools needed—and they were very effective. Even today it is common to see Andean people preparing fields with these same tools. Agriculture was done by both men and women, with men using the footplow and women the hoe. Harvesting also was done by both sexes working together, as it is today.

Wild Food. In addition to agriculture, the Incas used wild plants and animals to supplement their diet. Certain areas of each province were reserved as hunting grounds, although the inhabitants could request permission of the king to use them (Kendall 1973: 155). Deer and guanaco, a wild relative of the llama, were the main prey. Vicuñas, another wild relative of the llama, were caught for their extremely soft wool; they were released after shearing. The wool was spun and woven into clothing. Birds were killed by snares, slings, or the use of the bola, a series of leather strips with stones tied at the ends.

Fishing. Because the Incas were a highland group originally, they did not make significant use of ocean and lake resources. However, Pacific coastal groups caught fish and shellfish, which were an important addition to the diet. There are reports that the Inca king had ocean fish brought to him as a delicacy, using the messenger service along the road system (see below). Groups around Lake Titicaca fished the waters there as well and were allowed to pay tribute to the Incas in fish (Kendall 1973: 155).

Crafts and Craftspeople
As in many large-scale, complex societies, the Incas had a high degree of occupational specialization. Because of the exceptional skill indicated by many of the objects manufactured by the Incas, it is thought that the makers were fulltime specialists. Such specialization is also reflected in the presence of workshops at Inca sites where such individuals toiled. Three craft occupations deserve special mention: pottery, textiles (i.e., cloth), and metal working.

Pottery. Inca pottery is highly distinctive and very well made. There are several different shapes, but the two most common are a plate and a large jar with a pointed base and elongated neck. The latter was used

OTABA CALLE
PVCLLACOGVAMRA

An Inca aryballos, used for storing liquids such
as chicha.

for storing liquids, such as chicha. The designs on Inca pottery are highly repetitive; geometric shapes are common, especially on storage jars. The designs on the pottery used at administrative centers for feeding the local workers were uniform. This is because the Incas wanted to make sure the people using the pottery recognized the source of their hospitality (Morris and von Hagen 1993: 177). Thus it was important that the pottery be made in a highly controlled way. The Incas actually set up communities of potters whose sole task was to do this. There are Spanish accounts of people being moved to a community to produce pottery for that province (Julien 1982, 1988).

Textiles. The importance of textile (woven fabric) production to the Incas cannot be overstated. Producing cloth was the second largest industry in the empire, after agriculture (Morris and von Hagen 1993: 185). Three grades of cloth were made, each serving a different purpose. The coarsest weave was used for making blankets only, and the medium

QVNTA CALLE
CIPAS COVA

Spinning wool, using a spindle and whorl.

weave was for basic clothing. The finest cloth, called *cumbi cloth*, was carefully woven and of exceptionally high quality (Rowe 1946: 242).

Clothing of all sorts was made from a wide variety of materials—including cotton and the wool of wild vicuñas and domesticated alpacas and llamas. Cotton was utilized more often on the coast, where it grows readily and where it might have been domesticated during the late Preceramic Period. Several shades of color, ranging from brown to white, were grown and used on the coast. Wool textiles were more common in the highlands, because cotton does not grow well in the high altitudes and because camelids (llamas, alpacas, and vicuñas) are abundant there. The wool is easy to dye and spin; owing to its exceptional warmth and light weight, it is an ideal material for highland peoples.

Both cotton and wool must be spun into thread before being woven. This was done with a simple spindle and whorl. Starting with a ball of material attached to a stick, a woman (this was generally women's work) would twist some of it into a thread and wrap it around the spindle. The spindle whorl, attached to the end of the spindle, acted to keep the spindle rotating at an even rate to make the thread uniform in thickness. The spindle and whorl also acted as a weight to keep the thread taut. Women could spin thread while doing other activities, such as herding or visiting. The practice is still common in the Andes today. After spinning, the thread could be dyed or used in its natural color.

Weaving the spun wool into cloth involves combining two sets of threads, one long and one short, that are perpendicular to each other. The longer threads are called the *warp,* and the shorter cross-threads are called the *weft.* The process involves adding weft threads across the warp, one by one. By varying colored threads in the weft, complex patterns can be made. Weaving was done with a loom, of which two kinds were common. The first was a belt, or backstrap, loom. With this, the warp threads were attached at one end to a tree or post, with the other

A 33-year-old woman weaving, using a
backstrap loom.

end going around the waist of the weaver. The weft threads were added
by crossing them over and under the warp threads, then pushing them
snugly against the previous weft. To add more or less tension to the
weave, the person simply moved her body away or toward the post. The
second kind of loom was a standing loom, one that had a vertical frame.
It was used specifically for making cumbi cloth, the best-quality cloth
(Rowe 1946: 241). Additional materials could be woven into the fabric
as it was produced. The Incas added feathers and gold ornaments to
their finest cloths.

Cloth in Inca society had five important uses, in addition to its use as
clothing: (1) it was a form of identity by which to recognize where an
individual was from; (2) it was an indicator of prestige; (3) it was used
in ceremonial occasions as offerings; (4) it was given as official gifts to
conquered people; and (5) it was a form of payment for members of the
army (Murra 1962). When one considers the many ways that cloth functioned in the empire, it is easy to understand its importance to the Incas.

One early Spanish writer, Bernabé Cobo, noted that the Incas required
people to wear their native clothing wherever they were in the empire,
and that they were severely punished if they did not. This indicates that
the particular way of dressing was distinctive from group to group, as
it still is in many remote regions of the Andes today. For instance, the
kind of hat worn by individuals today mirrors Cobo's comments that
the most important insignias of identity were worn on the heads of men.

The wearing of distinctive clothing allowed a person's place of origin
to be recognized from a distance. Therefore it became much more difficult to leave one's group, because one would be immediately recognized
by Inca officials. Being that the Inca mitima policy was so extensive, the
wearing of identifiable clothing became an important source of control
over people's movements.

In a similar vein, designs were highly significant in the Inca prestige
system. Certain patterns identified the wearer as a member of a royal
panaca, and other patterns identified other social groups. Thus not only
could one recognize a person's place of origin by his or her clothing, but
one could also determine his or her social status. Therefore one would
immediately know how to act toward someone on sight.

Cloth had ceremonial and political uses as well. Virtually all sacrifices
to Inca gods involved the burning of cloth, especially cumbi cloth. It is
said that one hundred cloths of the finest quality were burned in sacrifice
to the sun every morning in Cuzco (*The Incas* 1979). Why was cloth sacrificed? It had an important role in the society, and people typically sacrifice what has value to them.

Cloth was also used in a political sense. When a group was conquered,
the Incas gave cumbi cloth to the vanquished leaders as a sign of respect
for them (Morris and von Hagen 1993: 190). By accepting the cloth, the

conquered leaders accepted their position of subservience to the Inca empire. Finally, soldiers in the army were given a specific amount of cloth as part of their pay, and there are accounts of rebellions when soldiers failed to receive their ration of clothing (*The Incas* 1979).

For the reasons just described, cloth production, like pottery manufacture, was carefully controlled. Cloth was frequently given as a reward for good service, so rulers and administrators had to have large quantities on hand. Therefore a large number of persons were employed by the Inca empire to make cloth. At the Inca city of Huánuco Pampa, one very large part of the site was dedicated almost exclusively to the production of cloth (Morris and Thompson 1985: 92). In the provinces, apparently there were villages dedicated to the production of cloth as there were villages focused on pottery (Julien 1988).

Metals and Mining. The Incas used metals for various purposes. Gold and silver were used extensively, but only for luxury items and ceremonial objects (e.g., llama figurines) that were often buried with sacrificial victims at the tops of mountains. The use of these two metals was restricted to the Inca nobility. The lower classes used copper, a soft metal that can easily be worked to achieve a variety of shapes, for items of personal adornment (e.g., large pins used for holding shawls closed), as additions to clothing, and for a variety of ceremonial objects such as sacrificial knives. On the other hand, because it is soft, copper is not good for making tools. The metal of choice for tools was bronze, a combination of copper and tin or arsenic. Bronze was used for axes, chisels, knives, tweezers, and war-club heads as well as jewelry and other objects (Morris and von Hagen 1993: 225–229).

There is surprisingly little written about native mining activities, perhaps because this activity was very quickly taken over by the Spaniards and converted to their own techniques. Gold, silver, and copper, the three main metals used, are abundant in Peru and Bolivia. Only gold is found in its pure form. Most gold was found in streams; it was obtained by washing the gravels in the streambed. Some was also found by excavating. One of the few descriptions of excavation indicates that the mines were relatively small trenches, capable of holding a single person only. Mines were between a few feet and 240 feet long, dug into hillsides. Where the hole was vertically excavated, it was only as deep as a man could throw the dirt out; when it became too deep, another hole was begun. Stones and deer antlers were used as tools to break up the veins of ore, and sacks of animal hides or baskets were used to carry the material out of the mine (Root 1949: 206).

Mines were worked only during the summer, to take advantage of the warmth, and the miners worked only from noon to sunset, to prevent exhaustion. Mine work for the Incas was done with m'ita labor (see below) drawn from settlements near the mines.

Silver and copper are found as ores (i.e., rocks with several kinds of materials mixed together). Once the ore was removed from the mine, the valuable metal had to be separated from the rest of the material. This was done by heating the ore. Different metals have different melting temperatures, and can be removed at different times during the heating process. Copper may also have been used without heating, as it is a soft material and is found in relatively pure deposits.

Because the use of silver and gold was restricted to the government, mining for these metals was carefully regulated. Copper was used much more widely and thus was unregulated. The ore deposits and mines were considered sacred places, and ceremonies were conducted in their honor (Rowe 1946: 246).

The Incas were familiar with a variety of techniques for working metals, including simple hammering, casting, smelting, riveting, and soldering. (In fact, many metalworking practices preceded the Incas.) For the making of jewelry, the Incas utilized inlaying and incrustation to achieve intricate designs. They often employed the finest craftsmen in Cuzco to make the luxury items for which we have glowing reports from Spanish sources. Unfortunately, few actual examples remain; most were melted down for shipment to Spain.

Other Crafts. Woodworking was a specialized activity, and there are reports from Spanish sources of "cup specialists"—individuals who made wooden cups, or *qeros*. Bone, shell, feathers, and gourd were also used in manufacturing.

Craftspeople. It is interesting to note that toward the end of the Inca empire there was a tendency toward greater specialization of activity. In the Chupachos province near modern Huánuco, entire communities were dedicated to a single activity such as pottery or cloth manufacture. Others included honey and bird collectors, featherworkers, salt producers, herders, gold miners, and coca growers (Julien 1993: 206–207). It is difficult to know to what degree this specialization was specific to Chupachos. Certainly pottery- and cloth-producing communities were present in other regions as well.

Taxation and Trade   Remarkably the Inca taxation system required nothing of conquered people but their labor: no one provided a single ear of corn or piece of cloth that they owned. The Incas used this labor to produce the food and materials that were needed to maintain the empire. Indeed, labor produced the huge surpluses of food that supported large numbers of craftspeople and the Inca nobility, as well as the even larger number of common workers who came to serve the empire. Labor enabled the Incas to build cities and temples and a highway that was one of the largest of the prehistoric world, and to expand the agricultural systems of their subjects.

Agricultural Tax. As mentioned previously, all the land of conquered people was said to belong to the Inca king. The conquered people then were required to work the land. The Incas divided the food produced by each conquered people into three parts (Rowe 1946: 265): for support of the priests and priestesses of the Inca religion, for support of the large Inca political bureaucracy, and for use by the conquered people themselves. The Incas also claimed ownership of all animals and divided the conquered peoples' herds of llamas and alpacas by the same proportions. Apparently the relative sizes of the distributions were variable; in some regions the Inca religion received a larger part, and in others the state did. In these situations, it might appear that the Incas reduced the amount of food allotted to the conquered people by a substantial amount, which might have caused starvation. However, Spanish writers have noted that each household was given sufficient fields for its use and that each year the Incas evaluated whether a family's holdings were adequate (Cobo 1979: 213). Furthermore, the Incas used the labor of conquered people to build new fields and irrigation systems to produce additional food. So people probably were not forced to give up most of their food; rather, they likely had to produce more to satisfy the Incas' tribute demands.

M'ita: The Inca Labor Tax. The Incas required all taxpaying individuals (i.e., the heads of households) to work a certain period of time each year for the empire (Rowe 1946: 266). This labor was called *m'ita.* Each household, which was the unit of taxation, had to send a person for m'ita work. What they did depended on their skills. Many men were required to serve in the army. Others either transported food and goods from local fields to the Inca centers, or made crafts.

M'ita labor was organized in such a way as to minimize disruption in the lives of the worker and his family. When a person was called to do m'ita labor, other ayllu members were required to do his other work for the community. Involving the ayllu was determined in such a way that enough men were left at home to tend the fields and crops. The principal job of the curacas was to decide whose turn it was to work in the m'ita rotation. To illustrate:

> The Inca king decided a new bridge was to be constructed over a major river in the middle of a province. Inca engineers determined that 600 men would be needed over a period of 18 months. So the king decreed that 600 men should be called up from that province for the bridge construction. The governor of the province summoned the two curacas of 10,000 households and told them they needed to call up 300 men each. Each curaca then ordered his two curacas of 5,000 households to provide 150 men. In turn, each of these called his five curacas of 1,000 households and ordered 30 men from each. These officials each called two curacas of 500 to present 15 men each. The five curacas below them were ordered to call up 3 men

*from their 100 households! These 600 men worked for a period of time,
fulfilling the m'ita rotation, and then returned home. Next the process was
repeated to find another 600 men to work. This continued for 18 months
until the bridge was completed.*

It is important to note that although a large number of men were
needed, only 3 men out of 100 households at the ayllu level were actually
called, or 3 percent of the total. This shows how the Incas were able to
construct so many monuments in such a short time, yet still allow people
to carry on their lives with minimal disruption. It should be kept in
mind, of course, that while the 3 men from each unit of 100 households
were working on the bridge, others were doing different services such
as serving in the army, working in the mines, or acting as runners in the
communication system. In fact, because every man was required to do
some labor for the Incas each year, there are reports of unnecessary work
being generated simply to keep the workers occupied (Rowe 1946: 268)!

Even though most of the labor of the empire was done by the m'ita
workers, certain tasks were too specialized to be left to unskilled labor—
such as the production of luxury items (e.g., cumbi cloth, gold and silver
working). The Incas created fulltime positions that were the equivalent
of civil servants to do these. The positions were hereditary, that is, passed
down from parent to child. These individuals were exempt from m'ita
work and normally spent their time at Inca centers. Considered the best
skilled workers, they produced goods exclusively for the Inca nobility,
not for general use. Crafts used by the lower classes were produced at
the specialized centers in each province mentioned previously or by each
household.

There were two other categories of fulltime workers. One category,
yanacona, were servants and personal attendants of the nobility. Some
were selected at an early age for this job; others became yanaconas by
royal decree and worked the fields of Inca kings and other nobility. The
latter were selected from among the best and brightest of the conquered
subjects. Sometimes the yanaconas were given high positions in the government in gratitude for services rendered to an Inca king (Rowe 1982:
101). Like other professions, yanaconas were hereditary positions.

The other category of fulltime workers was the *acllyaconas*, or Chosen
Women. Selected from among conquered peoples in the provinces and
from among noble families in Cuzco, they did a series of important jobs
for the empire. They were selected for their physical attractiveness at
around age 10, then were sent to schools where they learned spinning
and weaving, cooking, chicha making, and other domestic activities. In
the provinces there was a hierarchy of these women based on their physical perfection and social rank (Silverblatt 1987: 82). The most perfect
were sacrificed to the Inca gods (see Chapter 5, Religion). Next were

PRIMER·CAPÍTVLO DELASMŏIAS
ACLLA·COIAS

Chosen Women (acllyacona) spinning thread,
under the supervision of a mamacona.

women, also of high beauty, who might have been daughters of local curacas. They were taken to Cuzco and made attendants at the most important temples or became secondary wives of the Inca king. Many served as attendants to lesser Inca gods or were given as wives to lower-ranking curacas. Some became *mamaconas,* or teachers of other Chosen Women at Inca centers. Most Chosen Women probably remained in the provincial centers near their homelands. Daughters of the Cuzco nobility could also become Chosen Women and serve the same purposes: they became wives, priestesses in the temples, or mamaconas.

The Chosen Women apparently served a very important economic role, being in charge of producing the large quantities of cloth used by officials of the empire. They also prepared the food and chicha used at government installations for serving the m'ita workers, and perhaps they even provided entertainment. As a luxury commodity they were also given as favors by nobles to others, including conquered leaders, as a way of cementing alliances and social relationships. For these reasons the Chosen Women were very strictly controlled by the government. They were like slaves in the sense of having no personal freedom, but they were more highly regarded in that their services were respected by the Incas.

Yet another group of tax-exempt specialists was the mitima workers who were sent to live and work in areas away from their homelands, either voluntarily or by force. Typically they performed agricultural work. Some mitima, however, were fulfilling their obligations to the state. Given the enormous demands of the empire for food, the mitima contributions should not be underestimated.

The Quipu: Knotted Accounting Cord. One of the greatest challenges facing the Incas as they expanded their empire was how to coordinate all the activities of their 10 million or more subjects, in particular how to keep track of the movements of goods and people throughout the empire. In modern times this may be handled through computers; prior to the machine age it was done by accountants writing down the numbers of people and goods. However, the Incas never developed a form of writing that could be used for governing their empire. What they did have was a sophisticated knotted cord device called a *quipu.*

A quipu is a set of strings with knots tied at various lengths. The kind of knot used indicated the number, and its position along the string indicated whether it was a unit of 1 or 10 or 100 or 1,000 or higher. The strings hung from a main cord, and their location along the cord probably indicated what category was being recorded—for example, people, llamas, corn (Ascher and Ascher 1981). Some quipus have been recovered with hundreds of strings. The quipu had the advantage of being portable, because it could easily be rolled up and stored.

As might be suspected, there was a special tax-exempt class of accountants schooled in the use of quipus. These people went out among the ayllus and kept close records of the flow of goods and services throughout the empire's provinces. They must have worked closely with zthe curacas to determine how many goods had been used or produced, and how many people were needed for certain tasks. Quipu officials also kept census data for the empire, although this information was not written down by the Spaniards and is thus lost to us today.

Trade and Commerce. Trade between people in the Inca empire was virtually nonexistent, as all aspects of the economy were controlled by the Incas. However, within provinces the people were allowed to have fairs at which they could exchange goods (see Economy discussion on p. 41). These goods must have been nonluxury items, because the Incas held a monopoly on luxury items. Local fairs continue today in many highland regions.

Along the borders of the empire the Incas did participate in exchange

CÕTADOR·MAÍOR·ÍTE3ORERO
TAVANTIN·SVIO·QVÍPOC
CVRACA·CON ☩ DOR·CHAVA

con tador ykipoues   con tador

An Inca accountant with a quipu in his hand
and a counting tray at his feet.

with outside groups, but often merely as a prelude to conquest. Frank
Salomon has studied the interaction of the Incas in Ecuador along their
northern boundary with non-Incas, and he has found that they continued
local practices of exchange in their early stage of contact. These ex-
changes were modified into the pattern of Inca control after a group was
assimilated or conquered (Salomon 1986).

ENGINEERING AND ARCHITECTURE

The Incas were master engineers, as evidenced in many of their constructions. Not only are many of their buildings still standing after almost 500 years in one of the most volcanically active regions of the
world, but their irrigation systems continue to function and their terraces
continue to support fields of corn, potatoes, and other products. In a

Inca stonework in
Cuzco, showing
superb fitting of
stones without
mortar or cement.

recent severe earthquake in the Colca valley of southern Peru, virtually
all the houses in the town of Macas were destroyed. The only ones left
standing were those that had been built by the Incas, who apparently
knew better than the people of today the most firm ground on which to
build (Pablo de la Vera Cruz, personal communication 1991).

Public and Private Architecture The Incas are probably most famous for their method of fitting building stones so closely together that one cannot slip even a knife blade between them. This technique was only one of several used by the Incas, and was reserved for the most important buildings, such as temples, administrative structures, and kings' residences. More common techniques were used for most other buildings, and these are often much less recognizable as Inca in origin (Niles 1987). Yet Inca architecture, be it of high or low quality, has common features that do make it identifiable.

Types of Masonry. Inca constructions were most often made of stones collected from fields and then laid in mortar. *Adobe,* or mudbrick, was also used, although in the rainy highlands this material is less well preserved. To cover the rough appearance of either fieldstone or adobe, a layer of mud or clay was put on the walls and then painted.

Inca masons building a structure of rectangular cut-stone blocks.

The best-known Inca buildings are made of *fine masonry,* that is, of carefully shaped stones that fit snugly against their neighbors. To achieve walls of exceptionally smooth and uniform appearance, the Inca stoneworkers used tools of other harder stones and bronze chisels. Sometimes the stones were shaped into roughly square or rectangular forms, then used much like bricks. This method appears to have been reserved for the most important buildings. Sometimes the stones were left in irregular shapes but were worked along the edges to fit together tightly. This technique was used more often when very large stones were needed, as in terrace walls or riverbank constructions (Hyslop 1990: 15).

All forms of fine masonry involved enormous effort, because the fitting was accomplished by pounding and grinding the edges with harder stones or bronze chisels until they fit. Although there is no mystery about how Inca stoneworking was done, it is not generally appreciated how tedious and slow the work must have been. Very likely the fine stoneworking was a craft done by specialists, as were pottery and weaving. However, a large number of unskilled workers must have helped quarry the rocks, move them, and raise them into position. Earthen ramps were used to raise the large stones if more than one row was needed. This activity indicates how enormous a labor force the Incas were able to mobilize.

Structures. Although it might be very large or very small, the fundamental Inca structure was a rectangular building with a single room (Hyslop 1990: 5). Usually there was one door in the middle of a long wall, although there might be more than one if the room was very long. Most Inca buildings contained a single floor. If the building was on a very steep hillside, a second floor might be added and entered from the rear and above (Gasparini and Margolis 1980). In the area around Cuzco, two- and even three-story buildings were also built, although the latter are very rare (Rowe 1946: 228). The roofs were made of thatch. Highland structures almost always had steeply sloping roofs, which allowed rain to run off. Most Inca buildings were rectangular, but other shapes were sometimes used, including round and U-shaped.

Rectangular structures were typically grouped together into a *cancha*, a compound of three or more buildings surrounding an open patio. The compound was enclosed by a wall. Like the basic rectangular building, the canchas could be small (with few buildings and a small patio) or very large (with more and much bigger structures enclosing a much larger space).

The canchas apparently served a variety of purposes. Many were living quarters, but others might have been used for temples or craft production areas (Hyslop 1990: 17). The buildings within the cancha may have served different purposes. It is suggested that when a cancha was used as a residence, the group occupying it was probably an extended family (Rowe 1946: 223).

Another distinctive Inca building was the *callanca*, or Great Hall. As the name implies, it was a long rectangular building—but like most Inca structures, it had no interior walls. Callancas often had multiple doors. These buildings are usually found around Inca plazas, with doors opening onto the plazas. It is uncertain what these structures were used for, although excavations in them typically uncover little trash of any kind

(Morris and Thompson 1985: 89). They may have been used as temporary residences for people in the Inca centers outside of Cuzco, although the ones in Cuzco itself were probably used for ceremonies (Hyslop 1990: 18).

An interesting multi-purpose structure found in Inca settlements is the *ushnu*, or central platform. This is usually found in the center of important state institutions, either in the middle of the main plaza or off to one side (Hyslop 1990: 69). It was used in rituals, as a review stand, and as a place where the Inca king could meet conquered leaders. Ushnus are only found at Inca centers built to administer conquered provinces, and in Cuzco. Thus, like other Inca public buildings, they were symbols of Inca dominance over conquered people.

The second most noted feature of Inca architecture is its use of trap-

Inca king sitting on top of an ushnu in Cuzco.

ezoids. In the vicinity of Cuzco, most openings to buildings, doors, windows, even interior niches are trapezoidal, with the widest part at the bottom. The significance of this shape is unknown. In areas south of Cuzco, rectangular forms appear. The trapezoid disappears in the regions of the Inca empire south of Lake Titicaca (Hyslop 1990: 9–10).

Housing. The typical house of the Incas around Cuzco was a rectangular, single-roomed building with one door and no windows. It was built of rough fieldstone, then plastered and painted. The roof was steeply sloped and had a thatch covering. Three or more of these buildings were grouped into a cancha, which was occupied by an extended family. Both royalty and commoners lived in such structures, although those of the royalty were no doubt considerably larger and made of finer masonry.

Outside of Cuzco in the conquered areas, houses tended to be different. Because it was the Inca custom to leave a conquered people as unchanged as possible, most continued occupying the kinds of houses they had prior to their subjugation. Thus in the provinces houses might have been round or rectangular. The Wanka, a group living in the central highlands due east of modern Lima, had compounds of round houses, as did groups of the Huánuco area. Construction techniques might also be different. On the coast, where rock is not as abundant as in the highlands, adobe was a more common building material; and because rain seldom fell, roofs were flat and made of woven reeds.

In fact, it is sometimes difficult to identify a settlement as belonging to the Inca empire, because its houses and tools might be the same kind as were used prior to the Inca conquest. Sometimes the only way one can identify the presence of an Inca official is by the presence of a rectangular house among round ones or by the presence of Inca pottery (Malpass 1993b).

Public Buildings. Inca public buildings are easily identified by their shapes and fine masonry, and architectural features like trapezoidal doors and niches. However, fine masonry is much more common in the Cuzco area than elsewhere in the empire; there is virtually none in the southern or western part of the empire (Lynch 1993: 131). It is found where the Incas built structures of such importance that they merited the extra effort. In administrative centers built in conquered territories, it might have been deemed necessary to construct a series of large buildings of fine masonry to impress the conquered people with the power and capability of the Inca kings. In such places, callancas and canchas served as visible symbols of Inca power.

Temples. Inca temples were also important structures—and none so much as the Coricancha, or Temple of the Sun, in Cuzco. This may well have been the most important building in the empire. In fact, the walls that are still preserved (the Spaniards built a church on top of it) are

Sacsahuaman, above Cuzco. This structure, often called a fortress because of
the defensive nature of the outer walls (shown here), was probably used for
several purposes.

among the finest examples of Inca stoneworking anywhere. Many other
temples existed in Cuzco but few survived the Spanish Conquest, one of
whose chief aims was to completely obliterate the Inca religion.

Sacsahuaman. Another structure of importance in Cuzco was Sacsahuaman, the huge architectural complex located on an imposing hill to
the north of the city. It is said that 30,000 men worked on the structure.
Some of the largest stones ever worked and moved by the Incas are
located in the walls here, the largest being over 4 m (13 ft) high. The
importance of the structure is indicated by the fine masonry used in its
construction. The purpose of the structure is unknown, although it probably served different purposes. It is often considered a fortress because
of the layout of its impressive walls, yet early Spanish writers have suggested it also had religious functions, and others have noted that large
quantities of goods were stored there.

Town Planning. Where they were built from the ground up and not
within a conquered town, Inca settlements share certain characteristics

that indicate they were carefully planned. However, the patterns of Inca-built settlements are sufficiently different to suggest the Incas had no one standard to which all towns had to conform. Because several of the early Spanish writers have reported that the settlements were modeled on Cuzco, it is appropriate to describe the layout of the capital.

At the height of its power in the early 1500s, the valley of Cuzco might have had a population as high as 100,000 (Hyslop 1990: 39). Although it predates the ninth king, Inca accounts indicate that Pachacuti had rebuilt the city in the layout that it had when the Spaniards arrived. John Rowe (1967) notes that the city had the form of a puma, or mountain lion, with the head being the fortress of Sacsahuaman located on a hill above the city to the north, and the tail being the section of the city that narrowed to the south between two rivers. Pachacuti ordered the two rivers straightened for this purpose.

Many Spanish writers have noted that the region around and including Cuzco was set up to be a small-scale model of the Inca empire itself (Hyslop 1990: 64). Therefore it consisted of Inca-by-blood, Inca-by-privilege, mitimas, and many representatives of conquered groups. People of various occupations resided there, fulfilling both permanent and temporary labor obligations to the Incas.

The city comprised several sectors that were occupied by these different groups. The central sector was the most important, being occupied by the Incas themselves. The focus of this sector was two plazas, one of which was covered to a depth of several inches with sand brought from the Pacific Ocean (Hyslop 1990: 37). Many important buildings were located around these plazas, including a workplace for Chosen Women, several callancas, and the residences of Inca kings, other nobility, and royal panacas. Sacred shrines, storehouses, and temples were also located in the central part of Cuzco, including the Coricancha.

Surrounding the central sector was a zone reserved for agriculture. This area no doubt also separated the Inca nobility from lower-status groups living farther out from the center of town. Beyond the agricultural lands were several districts occupied by people who were not Inca: conquered leaders from the provinces, their sons and servants, and mitima from all over the empire. The latter were often craftspeople who were there to serve the Incas (Hyslop 1990: 63). Farthest out from the center of town were the settlements of the Inca-by-privilege.

Thus the Inca capital was more an aggregation of small settlements separated from the central sector by field systems than a city of continuous streets, like modern ones. It is this very large area that had a population of 100,000; the population of the central sector was no doubt much less.

Other Inca settlements were based on (1) a grid pattern, whereby streets cross each other at 90-degree angles, much like in modern cities,

Guaman Poma's map of the center of Cuzco
showing the two main plazas, the Huatanay
River, houses, and shrines.

or (2) a radial pattern, like the spokes of a wheel (Hyslop 1990: Ch. 7). The grid pattern is less common and is found mostly in regions around Cuzco. It appears to be associated with land that is relatively flat. Plazas are always found, but they are not in the center; rather, they are most often located at one end or side of the settlement. The central sector of Cuzco is laid out on a grid pattern, but the outlying settlements are organized on a radial pattern.

According to John Hyslop, a specialist in Inca architecture and settlement planning, the central sector of Cuzco may have had 20 different units defined by the intersection of the different streets. It is interesting to note that other Inca gridded settlements also have 20 or 40 units, suggesting they may have been laid out following the central sector of Cuzco as a model (Hyslop 1990: 202). The fact that the grid pattern is found close to Cuzco also suggests that it may have been the earlier model, used before the major conquests of the empire began.

Radial, or spoke-like, patterns are more widespread than grid patterns, and most of the best examples are found far from Cuzco. Thus the pattern may have become more common as the empire expanded; it may have been the preferred later model. However, a radial pattern is also found in Cuzco itself, where the grid pattern becomes a radial one as one leaves the central sector for the outlying settlements. The radial system may be based on a religious *ceque system* (see Chapter 5).

Radial patterns are typical of Inca administrative centers in provincial areas. One key feature is that they all radiate from a single point, typically an ushnu platform in the center of a plaza. This suggests that the point of origin was highly symbolic; the presence of an ushnu, which was a ritual structure, supports this interpretation. The ceque system of Cuzco also emanates from a single point, the Coricancha. Why it does not begin at the ushnu in the main plaza is uncertain.

The use of a radial pattern, and its association with the religious ceque system, suggests that the Incas used it as a formal model for settlements in conquered regions. It duplicated the royal capital at Cuzco and expressed some of the most important aspects of Inca society (Hyslop 1990: 221–22).

Private Estates. A special kind of settlement in the ınca empire was the private estate. This comprised lands and associated structures that belonged to a particular person or institution. Most of the best-known ones were owned by Inca kings or people close to them: brothers, uncles, even favored concubines (Niles 1993: 147). Because each king had to find new land and wealth for himself, he developed his own new estates. Thus much of the agricultural land surrounding Cuzco was actually privately owned. As the number of kings expanded, new estates were founded in the adjacent Vilcanota-Urubamba valley. Other estates, however, were located in the provinces far from the capital (Julien 1993).

Most estates were founded to produce food for the owner. This produce was significant: the more important a person was, the more food and goods he or she was expected to provide to his or her workers, or as gifts. A wide variety of food was produced on the estates, although in the Cuzco region most estates were devoted to corn production (Niles 1993: 150).

Other estates were more like country residences for their owners—a place where the owner could escape from Cuzco for relaxation. Some of the most famous Inca sites, such as Machu Picchu, were actually private estates of this kind. They functioned like small communities with their own fields, kitchens, sleeping quarters, servants' houses, and shrines to the gods. Often the home of the owner was an impressive palace, showing all the hallmarks of a high prestige building. Susan Niles, an expert on Inca estates, suggests that estates were an important status marker for new kings and that their creation was carefully documented along with a king's conquests and other notable achievements (Niles 1993: 150).

One of the Incas' less-appreciated achievements was their development of significant agricultural systems throughout the Andes. As mentioned previously, the Incas reorganized conquered peoples to increase their production of agricultural crops, particularly corn. In the highland regions this was often done by constructing large groups of terraces and irrigation works. There are approximately one million hectares of terraced land in the Andes today, and studies in different parts of the Andes indicate that many of the terraces were constructed during Inca times (Denevan, Mathewson, and Knapp 1987). Although the use of terracing preceded the Incas, they often expanded on existing systems and improved them by adding irrigation (Malpass 1987). The Inca engineers' effectiveness in planning terraces is indicated by the fact that many of them are still in use today, almost 500 years after their construction.

Terracing and Irrigation Works

Inca irrigation and water management systems also were impressive. Irrigation canals were often many kilometers long, and sometimes they were stone-lined and covered. The Incas also straightened entire river channels in the region of Cuzco; and it is reported that the bed of the Tullumayo River, where it flowed through Cuzco, was completely paved (Rowe 1946: 233). Aqueducts to bring water over gullies and reservoirs to store water during the dry season were also notable features of Inca engineering.

The Inca road system was one of the largest in ancient times, being over 23,000 km (14,000 miles) long (Hyslop 1984: xiii). There were two main roads: a highland one and a coastal one (see Map in Introduction). Connecting roads between them linked major centers. The highland road ran from northern Ecuador all the way to Argentina; the coastal road started at the Ecuadorian border with Peru and ran at least as far as Arequipa. Another part of this road traversed the dry coastal desert of Chile.

The Road System

Design and Use. The wheel was never invented in South America, so all travel was on foot (see subsequent discussion, Transportation). Because the road system was designed for an empire without wheeled vehicles, it was very different from modern roadways. The road often ascended very rapidly, going directly up steep slopes, although zigzags were used on occasion to decrease the steepness. In some areas it was quite wide, as much as 25 m (82 ft); in other areas it was barely more than a footpath. Generally the road is wider where the land is flat, and narrower where it ascends or descends slopes.

The principal use of the road system was to improve communication between different regions of the empire, but it also served as a visual

A reservoir for irrigating fields.

symbol of the Incas' power and authority over their subjects. The road system was built and maintained by m'ita labor. Sections of it were built by earlier people, especially the Huari, who apparently were the first to construct an organized system of roads. However, the Incas greatly expanded these earlier roads and no doubt improved them in many regions.

Bridges. In the highlands, one of the major obstacles to any road system were rivers. Many deep, wide, and fast-flowing rivers required bridges. In areas where the rivers flowed through steep canyons, suspension bridges were constructed of ropes by the Incas. These bridges were hung from towers on either side, with a walkway placed across the thick ropes that held the bridge together (Rowe 1946: 232). Some of the bridges continued in use into the nineteenth century (Squier 1877), although they were rebuilt often as the ropes wore out. Two other means of crossing were pontoon bridges and simple planks across a narrow river (Hyslop

Inca storehouses at a provincial center. An Inca
accountant with a quipu is at right.

1984: Ch. 22). Where the road crossed swampy areas, the Incas built
causeways to raise it above water level.

Settlements. A system of settlements was constructed along the highways as the empire grew. Some were quite large, such as the city of Huánuco Pampa in the northern highlands. This center had over 4,000
buildings, including storehouses that could hold approximately one million bushels of produce (Morris and Thompson 1985). The site was used
for provisioning and housing the army, storing goods produced in nearby
provinces, serving as temporary residence for royalty passing through,
and providing large-scale production of cloth and other goods. Similar
centers, found along the highway system at irregular intervals, were important nodes in the empire's communication and economic systems.

In addition to the major cities, along the highways were a series of

CORE ON·MAJOR·IMENOR
HATVNCHASQVICHVRV
MVLLO·CHAS QVI· CVRACA ~

A chasqui, or messenger carrier.

smaller sites called *tambos*. These provided a wide variety of services, including housing for travelers, administrative control over a local area, craft production, and ceremonial activity (Hyslop 1984: 279). Tambos were said to be located a day's walk from each other, although in fact they varied from a walk of 2 to 3 hours to one of a long day.

For any empire spanning more than 5,000 kilometers, some form of communication system must be developed so that news can be carried from one end to the other (or, in the Inca case, from the provinces to Cuzco). For this purpose the Incas devised a system of messengers. Every mile or so along the road was a hut on either side of the road occupied by a messenger, or *chasqui*. When a runner neared the hut, the occupant came out and ran alongside him, heard the message to be passed on and perhaps took a quipu, and then ran as fast as possible to the next hut along the route. The hut on the other side was for messages going in the opposite

Communications

direction (Rowe 1946: 231). A message could travel about 240 km (150 miles) a day on this route, or go from Lima to Cuzco in three days. In comparison, Spanish mail by horse took twelve to thirteen days two centuries later! This is also how fish could be brought to the Inca king in Cuzco before it spoiled. Chasquis were selected from local villages and were part of the m'ita labor given to the empire. Runners served fifteen-day rotations for this occupation.

TRANSPORTATION

Goods were transported on the backs of humans and animals. People carried goods in a cloak or by a rope slung over the back and tied in a knot over the chest. Jars were carried by a rope that was passed through handles on the pot and tied over the chest or around the forehead, like any other bundle (Rowe 1946: 237).

The llama was the only pack animal used, but it was ideally suited to the Andes. Llamas can carry a load of about 80 pounds up and down steep slopes. Although horses and donkeys introduced by the Spaniards can carry heavier loads, they have neither the endurance nor the sure-footedness of llamas. Caravans of llamas were used for transporting items, with a large number of spare animals so that the loads could be shared. Llamas can forage along the route, so food does not have to be supplied for them except in desert areas.

In coastal areas and on Lake Titicaca, Inca subjects transported goods with rafts. Along the coast one-man rafts of reeds were made, primarily for fishing. Such boats are still used in the vicinity of Trujillo, but the art of making them is being lost. Farther north along the Ecuadorian coast, much larger sea-going rafts were constructed of logs that were used for trade (Bruhns 1994: 281–286). In areas farther south, in Chile, rafts were made of inflatable sealskins but were used primarily for fishing, not transport. In the area around Lake Titicaca, a small ethnic group called the Uru were specialized fisherfolk. They too used rafts made of reeds for their fishing activities.

Yet another mode of transportation used by the Incas was the litter, a simple device made of poles with a seat strapped between them. Litters were used for carrying people, but only members of the highest nobility. Litters were carried by chosen bearers who came from the Andamarca Lucanas group in the central highlands (Schreiber 1993).

SOCIETY AND POLITICS AMONG
CONQUERED PEOPLES

Life among conquered people is difficult to reconstruct because there are few historical records about them. Yet by looking at what archaeol-

A royal litter carrying the Inca king Huayna
Capac into battle.

ogists have recovered about the pre-Inca way of life and then comparing
it to the changes identified as a result of the Inca conquest, we can for-
mulate an idea about life in the Inca provinces. It is evident that the
Incas caused significant changes in some areas and almost none in others.
How significant the changes were depended on many factors, such as
the level of political development of the conquered people, the level of
their resistance to conquest, the resources available in the conquered
area, and how the resources and people were distributed.

A very well-studied group is the Wanka of the upper Mantaro River
region of central Peru (D'Altroy 1992; Earle et al. 1987). Throughout the
Late Intermediate Period the Wanka were engaged in fighting among
themselves, apparently over prime agricultural land. The main Wanka
sites during this time were located on high ridges and hilltops and were
defended by large walls. There were two classes of people: elites, or high-

status individuals, and commoners. There were no marked differences between the two groups. However, the elites are identified by their larger houses, finer ceramics, and access to high-status objects such as silver, copper, Spondylus shells (a kind of oyster with a deep-red inner shell that was highly prized for making jewelry), and feathers from tropical forest birds (Earle et al. 1987). Both groups probably had to provide their own food and goods. The Wanka had a typical highland economy of agricultural products and herding.

The Wanka fiercely resisted the Incas but were conquered by either Pachacuti or Topa Inca, probably around A.D. 1463. In the center of the valley the Incas built a very large administrative center, called Hatun Jauja, little of which remains today. Because the Wanka were no longer fighting among themselves, they could be more efficiently organized for food production. The Incas moved the Wanka away from their earlier towns and villages, making new settlements to increase corn production.

What did the conquest of the Wanka mean to its citizens? There were some advantages. First, it increased their security, as the threat of warfare from neighboring villages was eliminated. Second, when there were droughts or early frosts that damaged the crops, the Incas would loan the Wanka food from their storehouses to be repaid from the surplus of good years. Although there is little archaeological evidence, we may assume that the Incas allowed the Wanka to continue the worship of their deities, as they did other groups.

Nonetheless there were certainly changes that would have been hard, physically and emotionally, on the Wanka. They were forced to work much longer in agricultural activities, to produce food not just for themselves but also for the Inca state and religion. They had to provide m'ita service, much of which was probably used for building Hatun Jauja and the segment of the Inca road that passed through the former Wanka territory. Female members were taken from some families to become Chosen Women, perhaps never to see their families again. Other craftspeople might have been moved permanently to Inca centers or to Cuzco.

The Wanka leaders became low-level curacas. Although this gave them access to Inca status items such as cumbi cloth, it also meant they were required to choose people for m'ita service and to organize agricultural labor for the Incas. In addition, their sons were taken to Cuzco, where they stayed for schooling in Inca administration and lifestyle. Conquered leaders were required to come to Cuzco yearly, to report on their responsibilities. Even though this would have given them the opportunity to see their sons (it is not known if this was allowed), the trip was long and difficult and would have reminded them of their subservient status.

The region in the vicinity of Huánuco, in northern highland Peru, is another area for which there is information about the transition from independent area to conquered province (Grosboll 1987, 1993). In this region five different ethnic groups were living near each other, although it is not certain how distinct each was. In contrast to the Wanka, these groups had little social differentiation; there were no elites and commoners. They had leaders, but the leaders had little in the way of greater wealth or other advantages.

The detailed Spanish records for this region indicate a significant amount of disruption in the lives of the people of this area upon their incorporation into the Inca empire. The Incas reorganized some of the ethnic groups to make decimal units of 1,000 households. For example, 300 households of the Quero ethnic group were lumped together with 700 households of the Chupachus (Grosboll 1993: 50). This changed the local chain of command, placing Queros under the authority of a Chapachu curaca. In addition, it is apparent that many residents of this region were moved elsewhere, either temporarily or permanently (Julien 1993: 210). Almost one-quarter were moved to Cuzco itself. Others were relocated to specialized communities within the province. A considerable number of m'ita workers from other parts of the empire were also moved into the region, to increase corn and coca production.

As with the Wanka, local leaders apparently were incorporated into the curaca class and given gifts that set them apart from the other members of their villages (Grosboll 1993: 52). In fact, the residence of one of the local officials has been identified by the presence of a large rectangular structure with trapezoidal niches typical of Inca architecture—not of local structures, which were round. The presence of Inca pottery at this building further supports the view that it was an official's house and that he had access to special goods that other members of his community did not.

Like the Wanka, the life of the resident of this province involved more work after the Inca conquest than before. Chosen Women were taken to the regional administrative center, craftspeople resettled in special communities, and entire villages moved to improve agricultural production. The distinction between leader and commoner became more marked, as the Incas gave new responsibilities and honors to local leaders. Unlike the Wanka, many more people were moved permanently out of the region and significant numbers of mitima from elsewhere were moved in. Why this was necessary is unknown. It might be related to the suggestion by Julien (1993: 209) that this province was actually a private estate of Huascar's, won by gambling!

Even though the ethnic groups in the Huánuco area were less powerful politically before the coming of the Incas, they were no less resistant to Inca rule. In fact, the people of this region rebelled and had to be reconquered (Julien 1993: 205). In contrast, the more powerful groups (e.g., the Chimu) did not offer the same resistance after their initial conquest. Most likely the Incas took more care in safeguarding against such rebellions among the more powerful conquered societies.

In summary, political and economic activities under the Incas were very different for conquered subjects. The common person must have worked more, because both men and women had obligations to the Inca empire. Some people were moved from their homelands, either as a group or individually, sometimes never to see friends and relatives again. Girls selected to become Chosen Women were taken from their families and became both workers and commodities of the empire. Although they were apparently well taken care of, they were uprooted from their families and moved to a strange town and required to live with others whom they did not know. Although friendships probably developed between these women, they never knew when they might be given as a wife to an Inca official or selected to be an attendant at an Inca temple or shrine. The same kind of alienated existence must have been the fate of craftspeople who were moved to Inca centers as well, although they could lead a more normal life of having a wife and children of their own choosing.

Some modern writers have tried to depict the Incas as a group who cared greatly for their subjects, providing them food and clothing, beer and entertainment in exchange for their services. In return, their subjects came and worked hard for their Inca masters and were materially better off because of their conquest. In fact, one can imagine that conquered peoples probably feared and hated the Incas. The evidence of resistance and rebellions suggests they felt very similar to how people today would feel in their circumstances. Many allied themselves with the Spaniards against the Incas. Their lives were generally much different than before their conquest: they were required to do much more work, often far from their homes, with family members taken from them. Having to ask a local official of the empire for permission to do almost anything must have been particularly hard to accept. The ways in which the Incas affected other aspects of their subjects' lives are the topics of the following chapters.

3

Private Life and Culture

Very little is known about the private and educational activities of the Incas and their subjects. More is known about the lives of the Inca kings, because few early Spanish authors had an interest in writing about the ordinary natives' daily life. Nevertheless some documents offer insights into this topic, especially the native sources such as Garcilaso de la Vega (1966 [1609]) and Guaman Poma (1936, 1980).

LIFE CYCLE

Although all humans grow and develop in a similar pattern, commemoration of life events differs from society to society. For the Incas, the most significant developments were the child's first haircut, puberty, marriage, and death. All marked important transitions in the individual's life, and the Incas celebrated them with important rituals.

No special event marked the birth of a child. A woman simply went to the nearest stream and bathed herself and the newborn. She then resumed her duties around the household. After four days the baby was placed in a cradle, where **Birth and Infancy** it spent most of its time until it could walk (Rowe 1946: 282). Garcilaso de la Vega, an Inca descendant, mentions that a woman never picked up her child, either to play with it or suckle it, lest the child become a crybaby (1966: 212).

It was an interesting custom of the Incas not to name a child until it was weaned from its mother's breast, around one year of age. This important event was associated with the child's first haircut. A great party

Baby in a cradle. The straps prevented the baby
from falling out when she was carried on her
mother's back.

was given for friends and relatives of the child's parents, with much
drinking and dancing. At the end of the party the oldest male relative
cut a small piece of the child's hair and its nails, and gave it a name.
Then other relatives cut off a lock of hair, and each gave the child a gift.
The nails and hair were carefully kept. The name given to the child at
this ceremony was not his or her permanent name; he or she received a
new one upon reaching maturity (Kendall 1973: 76).

Childhood was spent learning the activities of the household. When
boys were old enough and strong enough, they would help in the fields
and with tending animals. Girls would help with the many household
tasks of cooking, cleaning, making clothing, and probably taking care of
younger brothers and sisters.

Puberty   The end of childhood and the beginning of adulthood were marked differently for boys and girls. A girl became a woman at her first menstruation, and a ceremony was held to mark this notable transition. The girl was restricted to her house for three days, eating virtually nothing except a little raw corn on the third day. On the next day relatives assembled at her house, and she was bathed by her mother, who also braided her hair. She then put on new clothes and went out to serve her relatives food and drink. As at her first haircut, the most important uncle then gave her a permanent name and she received gifts from all involved (Rowe 1946: 284).

A common puberty ritual was held for all boys reaching the age of 14, although the event only roughly coincided with the onset of puberty for the participants. For boys of the royal class living in the capital of Cuzco, the ritual took place in December at the same time as the Capac Raymi festival (see Chapter 5, Religion). The ceremony actually was a series of activities spread out over three weeks, with preparations lasting a good deal longer. Mothers had to prepare fine new garments to be worn at the different activities, a task that must have begun months in advance.

In November the boys made a pilgrimage to the sacred mountain of Huanacauri, located outside Cuzco. The purpose of the trip was to ask the spirit of the mountain for permission to perform the puberty ceremony. Each boy brought along a llama, which was sacrificed by slitting its throat. The llama's blood was smeared on the boy's face by a priest. Then each participant was given a sling to signify his new status as a warrior. Much dancing followed; and the boys had to do certain chores, such as collecting straw for their relatives to sit on and chewing the corn for preparing the chicha for the ceremonies to come (Cobo 1990: 149).

During the puberty ceremony the boys again made a pilgrimage to Huanacauri to make more sacrifices of llamas. The boys were whipped on their legs by relatives on the return home, as a means of making them strong and brave. The participants then performed a sacred dance, after which they drank some of the chicha they had helped to prepare previously. A week of rest was followed by another series of sacrifices, beatings, and dancing at the hill of Anahuarque, located near Huanacauri. The boys then participated in a race from the top of the hill to the bottom (the race often resulted in falls, some of them serious). At the end, each boy was given chicha by girls from the same royal class (Cobo 1990: 131).

The final part of the puberty ceremony involved a trip to other hills near Cuzco where the boys were given loincloths, formally marking them as men. Then the boys traveled to a sacred spring called Callispuquio, where relatives gave them their weapons: the most important uncle gave a shield, a sling, and a mace. Other relatives gave gifts and advice on how to act as a man and as a proper Inca. The final activity was the piercing of the boys' ears for wearing the earplugs that were the hallmark of Inca nobility. This marked the participant as a warrior (Cobo 1990: 133).

Similar rituals, although probably less elaborate, were conducted at the same time of year in provincial capitals—again, for boys of the noble class. The special ceremony for noble boys indicates the importance of becoming a warrior and a member in good standing of Inca society. No doubt the rituals also served to create special bonds between the participants.

Marriage Inca nobles and other privileged individuals could have more than one wife, although it is uncertain how many nobles other than the king actually had multiple wives. There was always a distinction between the principal wife and secondary ones. The principal wife was married in a ceremony, whereas the secondary ones were simply taken into the household. A secondary wife could not become a principal wife even if the original principal wife died. This custom prevented jealousy and perhaps even murder of a principal wife by secondary wives.

Kendall (1973: 84) notes that one of the duties of a secondary wife in a large household was to be a nanny for the legitimate sons of the father. After a son reached puberty, she became responsible for teaching him about sex, including having intercourse with him. Even after he married, the secondary wife remained with him and served the customary duties of that position.

The Incas believed that all their kings were directly descended from Inti, the Sun, the principal god of the Incas. Therefore the kings were considered to be divine. For this reason it was important to keep the bloodline of the kings as pure as possible. To ensure this, among the later Inca kings the principal wife, or *coya*, always had to be a full sister of the king. However, the king could also have as many other wives as he wished, and it was from those wives that the members of the panacas were conceived. For non-royal ayllus, marriage to a sister was not necessary because the founding members were not divine.

Apparently, marriages were arranged either by the couple themselves or by parents (Rowe 1946: 285). Women married between the ages of 16 and 20; men married around age 25 (Kendall 1973: 81). The marriage ceremony itself was relatively simple. The groom and his family traveled to the home of the bride, whose family formally presented her to them. The groom's family accepted her by placing a sandal on her foot; it was made of wool if the bride was a virgin or of grass if she wasn't. (The Spanish writers are silent about how this was known. It *is* known that virginity was not a requirement of marriage.) Then the families proceeded to the home of the groom. There the bride presented him with gifts, and their families lectured them on the duties and responsibilities of family life. As with other ceremonies, the marriage ended with a feast and presentation of gifts to the newlyweds (Rowe 1946: 285).

Kendall (1973: 82) mentions an interesting custom of the Inca nobility who resided in Cuzco. She cites sources claiming that all marriageable couples of the highest nobility lined up in the main plaza, and the Inca king paired them off and married them.

The final ritual of the life cycle was the funeral for the dead. Upon dying, an individual was wrapped in a shroud. **Death and** Part of the person's belongings were burned and the rest **Burial** were buried with the body. Mourners did a slow dance around the body before burial took place. Afterwards, women relatives cut their hair and wore their cloaks over their heads as a symbol of mourning, and other relatives wore black (Rowe 1946: 286). The period of mourning for nobles lasted one year. Nobles' funerals were more elaborate versions of the simple one.

Funerals of the kings were especially elaborate, including special treatment of the body and particular ceremonies. At death, the king's body was preserved—probably with herbs. The cold, dry air of the mountains also helped to naturally mummify the body. The eyes were replaced with replicas made of shell. Because the king was thought to be divine, he could not really be considered dead. Therefore the mummified body was kept in his palace, attended by his servants and family members, and brought out to participate in major festivals. The period of mourning lasted one year, during which special songs and poems were written about the king's deeds. These were performed by professional mourners, both men and women. To officially close the period, at the end of the year a special ceremony was held in which people washed away the pain of grief with sooty ashes (Kendall 1973: 69).

In contrast to modern societies, there were a variety of burial practices in the Andes. No tomb of a noble person has been found; all were probably destroyed during the time after the Spanish conquest by treasure hunters. Thus we do not know how the nobility buried their dead. In other areas of the Andes, funerary chambers called *chullpas* were built. These were round or rectangular free-standing structures. The bodies were placed in the chullpas, which could be used for several individuals.

WOMEN'S ROLES

Less is known about the roles women played in everyday life of the Inca empire than about men, but it is clear they were fundamentally important to most aspects of life. As discussed in Chapter 2, the Chosen Women had important economic, social, and religious roles. The lives of

An Inca king's mummy, brought out to
participate in a ceremony.

noble women were no doubt easier than those of commoners: they had
yanaconas to tend to many of the duties assigned to women. Yet fundamental activities such as spinning and weaving were conducted by all
women, of high class or low. Principal wives were in charge of running
the household and delegating duties to the secondary wives. Their task
was more managerial: making sure that the household ran smoothly and
that food and drink were prepared to high standards when important
individuals were entertained. It probably fell to the secondary wives to
do the preparations, especially in households that did not have yanaconas.

Women were in charge of other household activities as well, such as
preparing meals, cleaning, washing, and making clothing for the family.
They also cared for the children until they were old enough to contribute
to household activities themselves. This is one reason why infants were

strapped to their cradles for so long: to keep the mother's hands free for the other tasks she had to perform.

Although most Spanish chroniclers discuss the significant roles that men had in Inca society, recent interpretations of some of the reports suggest that women had important roles also (Silverblatt 1987). Women could own land and herds, because inheritance was through both the mother's and the father's side of the family. Thus they controlled certain economic resources, although to what extent is uncertain. Women certainly played key roles in religious activities, as many of the main Inca gods—such as the Moon—were female. The principal leaders for these cults, therefore, were women (Silverblatt 1987: Ch. 3).

MEN'S ROLES

Both men and women lived in their parents' houses until they married, at which time they set up their own household. If a son was a member of a royal family, he could live in Cuzco and have his own and his family's needs met through tribute to his panaca. Daughters of a royal household could remain with their panaca or marry into their husband's panaca. Many nobles also owned private lands, or estates, that provided the necessary income (food, principally). Thus, like the privileged in many societies, the sons and daughters of the wealthy and elite had their basic needs met by the state or by family means. They were also exempt from paying tribute or participating in the m'ita. A son of a member of the non-royal ayllu might become an administrator or other state official, such as a quipu accountant. He might also serve in the army. He might own land, although it is probable that yanaconas worked it for him.

EDUCATION

There was little formal education in Andean societies: children learned from their parents and older siblings. Because there was no system of writing, knowledge was passed on verbally. This could be done by anyone. An exception was the use of quipus, the specialized accounting system of the Incas.

The only persons who received any formal training were the sons of the nobility and provincial rulers, and the Chosen Women. Boys received a four-year education at a school in Cuzco, where they learned Quechua in the first year, Inca religion in the second, quipu use in the third, and Inca history in the fourth (Rowe 1946: 283). Teachers were called *amautas*, or wise men. Training was by practice, repetition, and experience. The amautas maintained discipline through threats and beatings—although these were restricted to a single beating per day, and that only ten blows to the soles of the feet!

Chosen Women were selected at around age 10 from among the conquered people. They were taken to the provincial capital to be schooled in the arts of spinning, weaving, cooking, chicha-making, and religion. The period of instruction lasted four years, after which they were taken to Cuzco and presented to the Inca king, who decided their fate. Silverblatt (1987: 63) notes that young women from both the provinces and nobility also received training, although not in a formal school. Rather, they were taught in the houses of noblewomen in Cuzco.

FOOD AND DRINK

A wide variety of foods were eaten by the Incas and their subjects. Most of their food was domesticated. The Incas grew corn, potatoes, oca, ullucu, quinoa, *tarwi* (a kind of grain), and squashes of several varieties. The main sources of meat were guinea pigs and ducks, although llamas were also eaten. Wild plants and animals were relatively minor contributors to the food supply. Fish was consumed along the coast and near Lake Titicaca.

Food was either boiled in a pot or roasted over an open flame. Soups and stews were the main dishes, and a wide variety were eaten (Rowe 1946: 220). The recipe for one of these, called *motepatasca* by Cobo (1890–1895: bk. 14, Ch. 4), consisted of corn cooked with herbs and chili peppers until the kernels split open. Another, called *locro*, was a stew made of meat, potatoes, *chuño* (freeze-dried potatoes), other vegetables, and chili peppers. As in the Andes today, chili peppers and other spices were often used to make food more flavorful. A kind of corn bread was also made, either by boiling it or baking it in the ashes of a fire. Corn was toasted for eating while traveling. Popcorn was considered a delicacy.

The main drink was chicha, a mildly fermented beverage made from any of several plants, predominantly corn. To prepare it, women chewed the kernels, seeds, or fruit and spit the pulp into a large jar filled with warm water. Enzymes in the saliva broke down the sugars in the pulp, allowing it to ferment over the course of several days. The longer the fermentation process went on, the stronger the alcohol content became. Chicha was the staple drink of natives throughout the Andes, but it also had enormous religious importance for the Incas, being used in all religious ceremonies. Cobo (1979: 27) mentions that water was never drunk unless there was no chicha or other drink.

The Incas ate only two meals a day, one in the morning at 8 or 9 o'clock and one in the afternoon at 4 or 5 o'clock. Whether certain foods were preferred for these meals is not known. The Incas ate sitting on the ground. Women ate back to back with the men, facing the cooking pots. Cooking was done in ceramic pots with pedestals or tripods placed directly in the fire. The Incas ate from flat plates, sometimes decorated with animal-head handles, and drank from tall cups made of wood or pottery. The only difference between nobles and others was that nobles used plates and cups made of gold and silver, rather than pottery (Rowe 1946: 220–221).

For special occasions people sat in two lines, corresponding to the two moieties. They sat on the ground, facing each other, with the most important person sitting on a stool at the head of the lines. The food was the same as at any other meal, and each family brought its own food.

Food and drink were stored in large pots or jars, typically with pointed bases. Household storage was done in bins of cornstalks plastered with mud, attic or rafter space, and mud-lined pits in the floor. Outside storage structures were made of adobe and were typically larger. Food from the harvest was stored in outside structures, then brought inside when its use was imminent.

Meat and fish were preserved by freeze-drying, a process also used to make chuño from potatoes. This procedure was commonly done in the winter, when it is cold and dry in the highlands. Potatoes were softened in water, then ground up and left to freeze at night. During the day when temperatures rose, the potatoes thawed and the water evaporated, drying the pulp. This was repeated until the potatoes were dried and would not spoil. Meat was cut into thin strips, pounded, then left to freeze at night and dry in the hot midday sun. This meat was called *charqui* (whence comes the term *jerky*). Freeze-drying enabled the Incas to store large quantities of food for imperial uses. Dried food also had the advantage of being easier to transport from its place of production to its place of storage.

The Incas used no intoxicants other than chicha, although they did use two drugs—coca and wild tobacco—as mild narcotics. Coca, from which the modern narcotic cocaine is derived, is a small bush that grows in the eastern foothills. The leaves were chewed with a small amount of lime to release the active ingredient, an alkaloid that mildly numbs the senses. Its use was restricted to the nobility and the religious elite. Tobacco, which was not cultivated but collected wild, was taken as a snuff and was used as a charm against poisonous animals (Rowe 1946: 292).

DRESS AND ORNAMENTS

Clothing for both men and women was very simple. Women wore a large piece of cloth wrapped around their bodies, tied at the waist with a belt, and pinned at the shoulder. Another piece of cloth, a mantle, was worn over the shoulders and fastened in front with a large pin, or *tupu*. Tupus were made most often of copper, but higher-class individuals might also have ones of silver or gold. Men wore a tunic over a loincloth wrapped around the waist and groin. Very similar to modern ponchos,

Inca noblewoman's clothing. Note the mantle
fastened by a tupu.

the tunic was a large piece of cloth doubled over and sewn along the
sides, with slits left for the arms and head. Men also wore woolen or
cotton fringes below their knees and around their ankles. In cold weather
men wore a cloak over their other garments (Morris and von Hagen 1993:
187–188).

Both men and women wore simple sandals made of woven wild plant,
cotton, or camelid fibers with an untanned leather sole. They were held
to the feet with woolen straps, which often were elaboratedly tied. Gold
ornaments were sometimes attached as well. Both men and women wore
headdresses, one of the main indicators of ethnic identity. In fact, each
ethnic group had unique headdresses. The Inca nobility also wore
crowns of silver and gold.

Even though the Incas' basic clothing was simple, it was often elabo-
rately decorated with brightly colored patterns that conveyed symbolic

Inca nobleman's clothing.

information. The designs on Inca men's tunics were highly standardized, reflecting symbols of membership in a particular group (e.g., membership in a royal panaca). Fine tunics worn only on special occasions might have designs from top to bottom, but the day-to-day dress tunic had a single band of square design around the waist, a band at the lower edge, and an inverted triangle at the neck (Rowe 1946: 234).

Especially prized by the Incas was clothing decorated with feathers from brightly colored tropical forest birds. Sometimes an entire tunic or mantle was covered; at other times only a portion. Plaques of gold and other metals were also attached to the clothing of Inca nobility as an additional emblem of status.

Inca men wore their hair short. The women let it grow long, parted in the middle. Women cut their hair only in mourning or as a sign of disgrace (Rowe 1946: 236). Men's hair was bound up in a specially woven band or a sling. The king's band was wrapped several times around his head and included a fringe, or series of tassels, that hung off the head-band over the forehead. His band also had a small pompom on a stick worn above it (Rowe 1946: 235). The fringe and pompom were emblems of the kingship: no one else was allowed to wear such articles. Women also bound their hair in a band of cloth, covered with a piece of fine cloth.

Jewelry was worn by both Inca women and men. Women apparently only used tupu pins and necklaces. The main piece of men's jewelry was the large earplugs that were the insignia of nobility. These had a shaft that went through the holes in the earlobes, and a round head with a diameter of about 2 inches. They were made of gold, silver, or other materials. Men also wore bracelets. For bravery in war, soldiers were awarded metal disks that hung around their necks and they also wore necklaces of human teeth taken from their defeated enemies (Rowe 1946: 236).

Little else is known about Inca ideals of fashion or beauty. Martín de Morúa, an early Spanish writer, states that Inca women tied strings above and below their knees to thicken the flesh of their thighs and shins, which was considered a particular mark of beauty (cited in Rowe 1946: 237). The Incas also apparently painted their faces, not for aesthetic pur-poses, but for war and mourning.

RECREATION

Little is known about the recreational activities of the Incas, probably because there were few times when people were not involved with the day-to-day activities of making a living. This was as true for children as for adults. For conquered peoples, it would have been doubly true.

Games and Sports Inca children played with tops, balls, and round pieces of pottery that were ground down to use as gaming pieces. Adults played games involving dice that had five numbers on them, not six. They also played games with a board and beans as counters, but exactly how the games were played is unknown (Rowe 1946: 288–289).

The Incas also gambled. Although Rowe (1946: 289) suggests the games were more for fun than to win, Julien (1993: 184, 209) mentions a game called *aylloscas* played by royalty (and perhaps by others as well) that involved wagering entire estates. This suggests that among the no-bility at least, some betting had high stakes.

Games of skill were also important in boys' training for the puberty rites (see earlier discussion on Life Cycle). Races and mock battles were undertaken to evaluate the youths' abilities to become warriors. Because participating in warfare was an important part of being a man, there is little doubt these games were conducted with serious intentions and the level of competitiveness was high. Reports of grave injuries to some participants point to this conclusion. Such games prepared the young men for the more serious activities of warfare.

ART

The Incas did not have a special medium that could be defined as art in the way that modern paintings or sculptures are considered art. What art existed is found on pottery, wooden cups, and cloth. There can be little doubt that art took a back seat to function. Inca art did not attain the levels of beauty that are attributed to the earlier Moche or Nasca cultures, but it is well made and attractive. This is probably due in part to the Incas' practice of bringing the finest craftspeople from conquered regions to make their artwork for them.

A common criticism of Inca art is that it is repetitive and lacks imagination with regard to subject matter. The Incas used a relatively small number of decorative elements, especially triangles, feather patterns, and squares. Plants, flowers, llamas, pumas, and human figures were also used, although very often in a stylized and geometric manner. This is partly because Inca art was mass-produced and partly because the purpose of the art was to convey symbolic messages about the Incas' power. The variety of forms and color combinations is certainly less than in earlier societies.

Some aspects of Inca art have not survived for modern appreciation. There were reports that the walls of the Coricancha were sheathed in gold and that the Inca king had a garden consisting of gold and silver models of plants and animals. It is also likely that houses were plastered and painted. The probable medium of choice for artistic expression was cloth, little of which survived either the Spanish Conquest or the ravages of time.

One can find an aesthetic quality in Inca stoneworking, in the way that the massive supporting stones were fitted with their edges recessed. The play of light and shadows over walls constructed in this fashion is pleasing. Susan Niles (1993: 157) has pointed out that many of the fitted stone buildings for which the Incas are famous were constructed by Pachacuti and that they reflect his personal perspective on the world; later kings had different architectural styles. This suggests that certain other artistic features associated with the Incas might be due to particular kings and their personal tastes.

MUSIC AND DANCE

Andean music today is enjoying wide popularity owing to its pleasing combination of instruments such as the Andean panpipe, harp, and guitar. The distinctive rhythms of the music, too, are very different from modern music. Yet it is uncertain how ancient this kind of music is. Certainly the guitar is post-Inca, having been introduced to the Andes by the Spaniards. But panpipes (made of pieces of cane cut to different lengths to produce different tones) have an ancient history in this area, so they may reflect a continuity of sorts between the past and present. It is not known if the music played on these instruments is as old as the instruments themselves.

Other instruments that the Incas likely used (known either through chroniclers' reports or archaeological specimens) include simple flutes, drums, seashell trumpets, tambourines, bells, and rattles. Music was apparently important in the entertainment of laborers who came to work for the Incas, in festivals, and in war. Kendall (1973: 50) mentions that musicians were trained to perform at the royal court and that several flutes were played together to extend the range of the music. Both Rowe (1946: 290) and Kendall mention the flute, which resembled the modern recorder. It was used for love songs and was the only instrument in general use throughout the Andes.

Dance was restricted to festivals or rituals; the modern idea of a dance as a purely social function did not exist. Sometimes dances were limited to men or women; sometimes both sexes were involved. As with dances at the royal courts of Europe during the seventeenth and eighteenth centuries, Inca dances were very formalized, with each participant essentially duplicating what the others did.

LITERATURE

All Inca literature was, of course, oral. It consisted of stories, songs, and performance pieces that were passed down verbally and thus were subject to change and personal interpretation. Rowe (1946: 320) notes that there were at least four kinds of literature: prayers and hymns, dramatic pieces, narrative poems, and songs. Prayers and hymns gave elegant praise of the Inca deities, very similar to the hymns of the Old Testament. Only two examples of dramatic pieces survive, and these are poor translations.

The majority of Inca literature were narrative poems dealing with religion, mythology, and history. Many of the myths discussed in Chapter 5 were passed down as narrative poems. Like the great Viking sagas, these were meant to be memorized word for word and repeated at public gatherings. Dramatic pieces were presented as part of public dances, by one or two actors answered by a chorus. Myths and dramatic pieces probably emphasized religious themes.

Songs and poetry (indivisible in Andean terms, because most songs are but poems put to music) apparently are the least changed of all literary pieces (Rowe 1946: 322). The subject almost always is love—especially lost love—with many references to nature. One of the oldest is a poem remembered by Garcilaso from his childhood (translated in Rowe 1946: 322):

> In this place
> Thou shalt sleep
> Midnight
> I will come

More would probably be known of Inca literature if the Spanish priests and officials had not so actively tried to stamp it out as reflecting pagan beliefs and customs. This is probably why poems are the least changed: they were the most likely to be passed on at the household level, and to be the least religious in nature.

PRIVATE LIFE, RECREATION, AND EDUCATION AMONG CONQUERED PEOPLES

Details of the private lives of conquered peoples are even more scarce than those of the Incas. It is certain they had their own life cycle rituals; many may have been the same as the Incas' because most aspects of daily life were likely shared widely over the Andes. We do not know if other groups had haircutting and naming rituals conducted on the first birthday. It is likely that members of conquered groups held puberty rituals, but they were probably much less elaborate than those described above for 14-year-old Inca boys.

Among conquered peoples, marriages were regulated by the Inca administrators. Even though individuals were free to choose their spouse-to-be, couples were not considered officially engaged until the Inca administrator of the province decreed it so. This occurred when the marriageable boys lined up on one side and the girls on the other. Each boy would choose a girl and place her behind him. If two boys wanted the same girl, the Inca official would discuss the matter with all involved and decide who should have her. The loser then would make another choice. When all couples were paired off, the official gave each the king's blessing; then they could be married following their own customs (Rowe 1946: 285). Such control of marriages by the Inca provincial officials apparently mirrored the custom in Cuzco whereby all marriageable couples of the highest nobility lined up and the Inca king paired them off. The more common practice was to have a single spouse; but if the man was a curaca, he might be given a second wife as a reward for good service to the Incas.

A wide variety of burial practices and rituals were conducted by conquered peoples. In the Cuzco region, small beehive-shaped tombs for commoners were often built in caves or cliff faces. In the Colca valley of southern Peru, burials were sometimes in the walls of terraces. In the region around Lake Titicaca, burials were in round or rectangular towers called *chullpas*. Most of these practices preceded the Inca conquest and were continued as part of the Inca policy of allowing conquered people to maintain as much of their prior culture as possible.

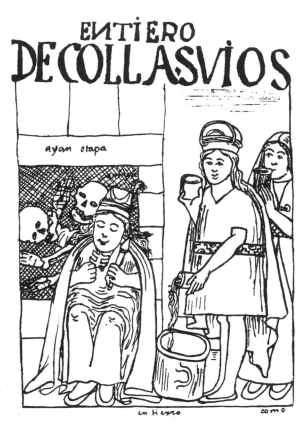

Chullpa burial in the Lake Titicaca region. An offering of chicha is presented to the gods during the interment of the individual.

Regarding the division of labor among conquered men and women, Silverblatt (1987: 4–14) notes that there were few gender-specific tasks prior to the Inca conquest. Although women were in charge of household activities, they also helped plant and harvest the fields, herd the animals, collect firewood, and do other tasks. Likewise men, although principally concerned with agricultural activities, also did many of the same tasks as women—even spinning and weaving if necessary. Thus little divided the male activities from the female ones; they were considered complementary and equal.

This changed following the Inca conquest. For the Incas, men were predominantly soldiers and women were cloth makers. This led to the beginnings of inequality between the sexes, because men participated in political activities as soldiers and administrators of the empire. It was the male leaders who were given positions of authority in the empire, not the women (Silverblatt 1987: 15–16).

Even though the Chosen Women were more important to the Inca empire's economic activities, the common women were important as well. Women were officially free from paying tribute, but they were part of a household that was obligated to do so. Thus when a husband or son was away fulfilling his m'ita obligation, women helped fulfill the other household obligations such as working the fields. In addition, any weaving or cloth production required by the empire fell to the women, because most weaving was a woman's occupation. In fact, all households were expected to make one cloth garment for the state each year; this would have been done by the women of the house.

Like their noble counterparts, conquered women were in charge of their household's food preparation, cleaning, and child care. A daily— and probably fairly strenuous task was collecting fuel for the fire. In forested areas, such as the eastern foothills, this might have been a relatively simple task; but in other areas, finding wood or llama dung to burn might take a few hours. It is likely that by Inca times, much of the native forest of the highland region had been cut. In addition, a woman returning from a long fuel-collecting trip might be carrying a child or two who were too tired to walk, as well as a heavy load of wood. There is little doubt that the woman was tired at the end of the day.

A man became eligible for the m'ita and other taxation upon marrying and setting up a new household. His family received a plot of land for its own use, which was reassessed each year to ensure that his family's needs were being met. In association with his community, a man had to work the fields of the Inca state and religion. He had to participate in the m'ita rotation, serving the empire in whatever capacity it requested. The three main activities were army service, public works, and mining (Kendall 1973: 85). If a man were particularly gifted in some craft, he might be selected to work fulltime for the empire as a craftsperson at a provincial center or in a special community in his own region of the Andes (see Chapter 2).

There was little possibility of improving one's status in life. The status of nobleman or commoner was inherited. However, a man could gain some measure of greater recognition through outstanding deeds in warfare. He could also become a foreman of 10 or 50 households, a position under the lowest curaca in the administrative hierarchy. The curaca position itself was usually reserved for conquered rulers and hence might not be available to a commoner.

Besides working the fields, one of a man's few domestic tasks involved making sandals for his family (Kendall 1973: 85). It is not clear how much men helped with the upkeep of the house or the raising of the children; very likely, it was not much.

Dancers from a province in Cuntisuyu. The costumes and masks were probably made of feathers from brightly colored birds.

The kinds of food and drink consumed by commoners were the same as the Incas consumed. The only difference was that the Inca nobility used plates made of gold or silver while commoners used ceramic or wooden ones.

It is probable that most non-Incas wore similar simple clothing of breechcloths and tunics. Cultural identity could often be determined by the kind of headdress worn; belts, slings, and woven bags might also have distinguishing designs specific to a local group (Morris and von Hagen 1993: 175–177). Thus cloth and clothing were more than functional; they constituted a visual communication system that allowed the Incas to identify the culture and status of an individual simply by looking at his or her clothing. This was particularly useful in keeping track of conquered people as they were moved around the empire.

Among conquered peoples, men's and women's hair styles varied widely. Unlike the Incas, many conquered groups practiced head deformation. Colca valley inhabitants were particularly noted for this, and the means by which they bound the head was a way of differentiating between local groups (Ulloa Mogollón 1965: 327). The deformation was accomplished by binding an infant's head to a board or between two boards for months or even years so that the skull would be flat, not rounded, as the individual grew. As far as scholars can determine, the reason for the head deformation was aesthetic: the groups found the artificial shape of the head pleasing.

It is likely that there was little difference in recreational activities between conquered peoples and the Incas. If any- **Recreation** thing, conquered people had less leisure time for socializing and playing: the additional labor requirements of the Incas would have taken up much of their spare time. Even today, subsistence farmers work from morning to night and have little time for leisurely activities.

Information from Guaman Poma (1980) suggests that dancers from the provinces often wore very elaborate costumes and masks, but little else is known about these customs. The artistic activities of a conquered people, manifest in their ceramics and other objects, might have been distinctive enough to be recognized in different regions. As discussed in Chapter 1, pre-Inca cultures of the Late Intermediate Period are characterized by unique cultural items, many of which could be termed artistic.

There were no schools for conquered peoples except the ones run by the Incas for the sons of local curacas and the **Education** training of Chosen Women. Education was entirely informal, based on observing one's older siblings and parents.

All in all, the private life of a conquered person was not significantly changed by the Incas except in terms of the control of marriage and economic activities. Families were kept together except when a person was selected to be a fulltime worker for the empire.

4

Science and the Calendar

It is uncertain whether the sciences of the Incas were any more sophisticated than those elsewhere in the world of the sixteenth century. Certainly the Incas' astronomical observations and calendars were not as accurate as those of other groups, for example, the Maya of Mexico and Central America. Yet they evidently understood many scientific and mathematical principles, particularly those needed in engineering, because they built masterful buildings that still stand today.

Regarding mathematics, it is known from studies of quipus that the Incas used a decimal system of counting. They also understood the concept of zero, because there is a place for "no units" on the quipus. However, the quipu could not be used like an abacus for quickly adding, subtracting, or multiplying. For these purposes, the quipu accountant used pebbles, grains, or a tray with compartments similar to an abacus (Rowe 1946: 326). Once the desired calculation had been made, the number could be recorded on the quipu.

The Incas must have utilized standardized units of measurement to plan their major construction works. For example, to be able to call up the proper number of m'ita workers for a project, Inca engineers must have had a system of determining the amount of work involved. Spanish writers differ on Spanish equivalents for Inca units of measurement, however, so it is uncertain how precise they truly were. Rowe (1946: 323) states that the units of length were based on the human body. There were units equaling the distance between the outstretched thumb and forefinger (5–6 inches); the palm (8 inches); the forearm, or cubit (18 inches); and the height of a man, or fathom (64 inches). The latter unit was used as a standard, and sticks of this length were kept for official use.

Units of area were also used, and here the standard was the *topo*. It apparently was a rectangular area roughly 50 fathoms by 25 fathoms (300 ft by 150 ft). This would be .8 acre. The topo was also the unit of traveling distance, approximately equal to either 4.5 or 6 miles, depending on the authority cited. A shorter unit was based on the pace of a man of average height, which has been computed as roughly 4 feet (a pace is the distance between where one foot is put down and where the same foot is put down again; that is, two steps).

To measure a volume of grain, the Incas used a large gourd that contained approximately 26 quarts. They had no standard unit of weight, although they did use a kind of scale to measure equivalents. Time was measured according to the distance the sun had traveled that day, and the hour of an event according to the position of the sun at the moment (Rowe 1946: 324–325).

The Incas made astronomical observations, but only of the sun, moon, and some constellations. Most astronomical bodies were considered to be deities, as they were to many ancient peoples. Hence the study of their movements was not as important as their veneration. For this reason the noted Inca scholar Tom Zuidema (1982: 59) states that it is impossible to understand Inca astronomy without discussing its relationship to the Inca calendar and rituals (see subsequent discussion).

Which celestial bodies were actually charted by the Incas is unclear. Modern studies have confirmed that the Incas made astronomical observations of the constellation Pleiades from the Coricancha at Cuzco and a building at Machu Picchu; and there is evidence of an observation point for the summer and winter solstices at Machu Picchu as well (Dearborn and Schreiber 1989). Other suggestions, including observations of the two main stars in the Southern Cross constellation, remain to be confirmed.

INCA CALENDARS

The Incas apparently used two different calendars, one for daytime and one for nighttime (Morris and von Hagen 1993: 180–183). The daytime calendar was based on the solar cycle and was approximately 365 days long. It was used for economic activities such as agriculture, mining, warfare, and construction. The movement of the sun was particularly important to the Inca agricultural calendar, being used to fix the days of planting. Four towers were built on the horizons east and west of Cuzco to mark the rising and setting locations of the sun in August, the time of planting corn and potatoes. The point of view was the ushnu in the main plaza of the city. When the sun rose over the first tower on the eastern horizon and set over the corresponding tower on the western horizon, it marked when the early crops should be planted in August. When the sun rose between two towers built close together farther south, it marked the time of general sowing in September (Rowe 1946: 327).

Zuidema (1990: 90) suggests that the Incas' nighttime calendar was developed to mark important ceremonies to the moon and stars (see below), which were sacred deities of the Incas. It had only 328 days, which equals twelve months of 27.33 days each. The latter almost corresponds to a lunar month, which is 28 days long.

There is an apparent problem with correlating the daytime calendar, based on the sun, and the nighttime calendar, based on the moon. The latter is 37 days shorter than the former. It is uncertain whether this correlation was important to the Incas.

Some scholars have argued that the Inca calendars could not have been based on such observations, as there is no good evidence of either the accuracy of the measurements or the particular astronomical risings and settings needed (Dearborn and Schreiber 1989). Part of this debate concerns whether the Incas recorded the solstices (the northernmost and southernmost points of the sun), the equinoxes (the midpoint between the northernmost and southernmost positions), and the zeniths of the sun and moon (the highest points in their orbits overhead). Zuidema (1990) and Ziolkowski and Sadowski (1989) suggest they did, but they base their arguments on the presence of important ceremonies falling on or near the days of those events. Dearborn and Schreiber (1989) argue that the observation lines are not sufficiently accurate to be sure that these ceremonies actually were celebrating the particular astronomical events.

What is clear about both Inca calendars is that they were used for determining when important ceremonies should be conducted, rather than simply for marking time. This relates to the Inca belief that nothing happened by accident but was always caused by a supernatural force (see Chapter 5, Religion). The agricultural activities and important ceremonies of the daytime calendar are listed below, given in terms of the modern months when they occurred (from Kendall 1973: 149–150, 198–200). See Chapter 5 for a description of the ceremonies. As stated previously, the Incas did not associate equal periods of time with each month; rather, they recorded the passage of the year in terms of the activities and ceremonies required of the gods at different times. Therefore the correlation of the Inca's calendars with the modern one is only approximate.

Daytime calendar	*Nighttime calendar*
December. Coca planting.	Capac Raymi (December). The boys' puberty ceremony was an important part of Capac Raymi, as were other rituals concerning the Sun. Tribute for the Inca state and religion was brought to Cuzco from the provinces at this time.
January. Weeding of fields.	Camay quilla (January). A continuation of some of the puberty ceremonies from the previous month was conducted, along with others to Viracocha, the principal god.
February–March. Harvest of the potato and other root crops.	Hatun-pucuy (February). Ceremonies were conducted to increase the corn and other crops.
	Pacha-pucuy (March). More rituals were conducted to ensure that the crops ripened properly.
April. Protecting the corn fields from deer, foxes, and human theft.	Ayrihua (April). Ceremonies honoring the Inca king were held.
May. Corn harvest.	Aymoray quilla (May). Celebration of the corn harvest was held.
June. Large potatoes were harvested and others planted.	Inti Raymi (June). Important rituals were conducted to the Sun.
July. Storage of potatoes and other crops; cleaning of irrigation canals.	Chahua-huarquiz (July). Ceremonies for the irrigation systems were held.
August–September. Planting of the corn and potato crops.	Yapaquiz (August). Sacrifices were made to all the gods, especially those associated with the forces of nature.
	Coya Raymi (September). The city of Cuzco was purified, and the sacred idols of conquered people were brought to pay homage to the king.

| | K'antaray (October). Ceremonies were conducted to ensure adequate rainfall. |
| November. Irrigation of the corn fields. | Ayamarca (November). The Festival of the Dead was conducted, with the bodies of dead kings brought out of their tombs to receive offerings and food. |

As can be seen, the nighttime calendar was more focused on nonagricultural ceremonies, although some months did have rituals in celebration of certain crops or related activities such as irrigation. The importance of corn to the Incas is indicated by the significance of the month of May in both calendars, which celebrated the harvest. The nighttime calendar, based on the moon's cycles, was important in setting the time of rituals. The Incas began their calendar in December with the Capac Raymi festival (Cobo 1990: 126).

Most pre-Inca groups had little need for standardized units of measurement and probably did not have them. It is likely that many conquered people observed the movements of the sun, moon, and stars and marked the passage of time by them, as the Incas did. Whether they had detailed calendars is unknown.

5

Religion

Inca religion was extraordinarily complex and constituted a fundamental part of Inca life. It emphasized formality and ritual; most activities were focused on agricultural practices, deity worship, or curing disease. For this reason the Incas had a very large group of priests who directed the formal religious practices of the state, and other individuals who could be consulted to help in matters of a more personal nature. Although religious and governmental bureaucracies were separate, it would be a mistake to say there was a separation of church and state. Few governmental actions were conducted without consulting the gods. In fact, the more important the activity, the more important the religious rituals that were necessary for the success of the venture. In addition, the religious bureaucracy depended on the state's conquests to provide food and supplies needed to conduct its affairs.

The conquering Spaniards regarded any religion except Christianity as evil and any other religious beliefs as devil worship. Thus they made an exceptionally determined effort to stamp out native religion. Nonetheless the Spaniards' interest in eliminating the native religion also led them to write a good deal about its practices and thereby pass on knowledge about it to future generations.

MYTHOLOGY

Myths are stories or legends concerning people and events in the past, especially ones that attempt to explain why the world or a people came to be. Myths of many societies are purely fanciful and have no basis in fact, such as those of the Greeks. Others may have some basis in fact, yet through countless years of telling and retelling have become more story than fact. Inca mythology contains examples of both. Also, myths concerning the origins of the world have been used by political leaders in many societies to justify the world order as they see it, especially in cases where there are marked inequalities between people. The Inca leadership certainly used their mythology for such purposes.

According to Rowe (1946: 315), all the Inca myths recorded by the Spaniards either explained where the Incas came from (origin myths) or described historical events. Whether other kinds of myths were held by the Incas is unknown.

The origin myth of the Incas justified their elevated social standing over other people. The founding father and first king of the Incas was Manco Capac, according to Guaman Poma. He came out of the earth from a cave at a place called Pacariqtambo, accompanied by three brothers and four sisters. Over a period of several years they traveled to Cuzco with a group of other people who were loyal to them, who also came from caves at Pacariqtambo (see Introduction). One brother became feared by the others for his exceptional strength and was sent back to Pacariqtambo, where he was sealed up in the original caves. Another brother stayed at the mountain of Huanacauri, where he originated the male puberty rites. He then turned to stone and subsequently became an important cult figure of the Incas. The two other brothers and the four sisters continued to Cuzco. Upon reaching the Cuzco valley the Incas drove a golden staff into the ground, which was the sign that this would be the place of their permanent settlement. A third brother turned himself into a stone field guardian. Under the direction of the remaining brother, Manco Capac, the Incas drove out the native occupants and founded the capital of Cuzco (Guaman Poma 1980: 80–87).

In another variation of this myth, Garcilaso (1966: 52–53) has Manco Capac and his sister (who was also his wife) travel to Pacariqtambo from Lake Titicaca, and then to Cuzco. After founding Cuzco, Manco traveled across the empire, organizing the ethnic groups and bringing them civilization.

The differences between these two versions are important, for they affect the social relations of the people who live with the Incas in the Cuzco valley. In Guaman Poma's version, Manco Capac and his sister originate in Pacariqtambo and are accompanied from there by others; these others become the Incas-by-privilege. Because they accompanied the original ruler to Cuzco, they too are given the status of "Inca." In Garcilaso's version, only Manco Capac and his sister come from Lake Titicaca; therefore the Incas-by-privilege were originally not "Inca." They were given the title later. The differences between the two versions thus reflect a difference in whether the Incas-by-privilege were Incas from ancient times or only became Incas when the royal couple arrived in the Cuzco valley.

An interesting perspective is provided by Brian Bauer (1992: 30). He notes that Garcilaso was the great-grandson of Huayna Capac and hence a royal Inca. From Garcilaso's perspective, then, the Incas-by-privilege owed their Inca status to his ancestors' having bestowed it on them. Guaman Poma, however, was from Huánuco and was therefore non-Inca. He saw the differences between the Incas-by-blood and Incas-by-privilege as one of degree.

Regardless, the clear implication of the origin myth is that the descendants of Manco Capac and the rulers of the Incas were the only noble Incas, and that others were subservient to them. The myth also justifies the Inca royal tradition of the king marrying his full sister (because Manco Capac did). In addition, it explains the existence of some of the shrines near Cuzco (where the two brothers were turned to stone) and the importance of the male puberty rites, because they were given to the Incas by one of the original brothers before he turned to stone (Rowe 1946: 318).

Another important myth describes how the earth began. The Incas believed in *Viracocha*, who was both the god who created the world and also a man who traveled the earth doing great deeds. Viracocha created the world and the sky with all its stars, and he brought the sun and moon out of an island in Lake Titicaca to light it. He then went to Tiahuanaco and formed people and animals out of clay. He painted each tribe's clothing differently. He gave them distinctive cultures and sent them into the earth, to emerge from it in their homelands. He then traveled throughout the world to see if everyone was behaving properly. Upon reaching Ecuador, he said farewell and walked out across the Pacific Ocean. Rowe (1946: 318) mentions how Garcilaso's version of the Inca origin myth seems to combine the myth of Viracocha and that of Manco Capac.

The myth of Viracocha explains in simple terms how the earth, stars, and people were all created by a divine being. In this respect it is similar to the version of God's creation of the world in the Bible. Rowe (1946: 316) suggests that the Incas used parts of the origin myths of other people—both of their own area and others, especially the Lake Titicaca region—to come up with one that explained the world as they had redesigned it.

GODS

The Incas had many *deities*, or gods, each with a particular area of influence and power. The most powerful was Viracocha, the Creator. This deity was neither male nor female. The Spaniards saw several statues of this being in various temples. One such statue, of solid gold, was in Cuzco; it stood about 4 feet high. The figure's right arm was raised and its fist was clenched, except for the thumb and forefinger (Rowe 1946: 293). Viracocha gave the other gods their authority. For this reason Viracocha was seen as a more distant power in the world, and the other gods had more immediate influence and control over the actions of humans. Thus individuals were more preoccupied with rituals for the other gods.

The three principal gods under Viracocha were *Inti,* the Sun; *Illapa,* the Thunder or Weather god; and *Mama-Quilla,* the Moon. Inti, the most powerful, was the god of agriculture. This god was represented as a golden disk with rays and a human face in the center. Illapa, the next most powerful, was associated with rain. He was usually depicted as a man in the sky wearing radiant clothing, holding a war club in one hand and a sling in the other. Mama-Quilla was a woman and the wife of the Sun. The Moon did not appear to have any particular functions, but the lunar cycle was the basis for the Inca nighttime calendar.

The gods of the sky, Inti and Illapa, were important to the Incas, no doubt because the sky was the source of both sun and rain for sustaining the crops. However, of equal importance were the god of the earth, *Pacha-Mama,* and the god of the sea, *Mama-Cocha,* both of which were regarded as female. Pacha-Mama was important to the Incas as agriculturalists, whereas Mama-Cocha was important to fishing groups residing near the ocean. Mama-Cocha was also the ultimate source of all water, including rivers, streams, and irrigation water. Hence she was important even to the Incas in Cuzco. Below these deities were various gods associated with stars or constellations that served different functions. For example, some stars watched over flocks of camelids, others over wild animals, and still others over plants and seeds (Rowe 1946: 295).

All major deities of the Incas constituted an official cult. Although the cult religious structures were called Sun Temples by the Spaniards (suggesting that they were used exclusively by the priests of Inti), they also housed the other deities and the priests who served them. Only the most important deities, such as Viracocha, Inti, and Illapa, were represented by images. Mama-Quilla, Pacha-Mama, and Mama-Cocha apparently had no images, and neither did the lesser deities.

HUACAS AND SPIRITS

Huacas   In addition to the deities just discussed, the Incas had a host of other beliefs in the supernatural. A pervasive part of Inca religious life involved the belief that many places and objects were imbued with supernatural powers. These supernatural features were called *huacas.* It is unclear whether the objects and places were

Inca king speaking to huacas, located in a circle. The huacas include ancestor mummies, mountains, rocks, and springs.

spirits themselves or simply the locations where spirits resided. Most huacas were local features of a settlement, significant to its residents only. Apparently the most common were springs and rocks. The Incas also had amulets that they believed held supernatural powers and that functioned like portable huacas (Rowe 1946: 297).

Particular reverence was also given to the bodies of the dead, who were regarded as huacas. The Inca kings' bodies were mummified after death and placed in temples, to be brought out during festivals and worshipped. Moreover, the dead Inca kings were considered to be active participants in the activities of their panacas, so their mummies were provided food and drink.

An unusual element of Inca religion was the *ceque system* (Zuidema 1964, 1990). This was a series of straight lines that radiated out from the

Coricancha in Cuzco, extending to the horizon and possibly beyond. Along the ceques were a series of 385 huacas, of which 328 served as a ceremonial calendar, according to Zuidema (see Chapter 4, Science and the Calendar). The ceque system served two purposes: to organize the geographic space around Cuzco, and to order the huacas according to the days of the year. For each huaca there was a special day when rituals were observed, and different social groups in Cuzco were responsible for the rituals of each huaca. The royal panacas were responsible for some of the huacas, and the non-royal ayllus and Incas-by-privilege were responsible for others. The system reinforced social distinctions between these groups.

Evil Spirits The Incas believed in both evil and good powers that could be manipulated for the good or detriment of humans. Evil spirits were dreaded by the Incas. Unlike the deities and huacas discussed above, who were generally considered helpful to humans unless proper rituals were not observed, spirits were always considered to be evil and intent on harming humans.

Afterlife The Incas' beliefs in an afterlife were akin to beliefs in a heaven and hell. Good people went to live with the Sun, where life was the same as on earth but there was always plenty of food and drink. Bad people went to live beneath the earth, where they were perpetually cold and had only stones to eat. The Inca nobility went to heaven regardless of character (Rowe 1946: 298). The Incas believed that the soul of a dead person protected its descendants from evil and liked its body to be brought out during festivals to be given food and chicha.

RELIGIOUS SPECIALISTS

Priests and priestesses associated with the official shrines and deities were fulltime specialists, supported by the tribute paid by conquered people. The fact that a third of the tribute went to the support of formal Inca religion indicates how many people were involved. There was a hierarchy of priests roughly paralleling the administrative hierarchy of the state. The priests were graded according to the rank of the shrine in which they worked. The highest-ranking priests were those who worked for the Sun. At the very top was a high priest, who was a close relative of the king and therefore related to the Sun. There was also a hierarchy of the individuals at each shrine: the attendants were subservient to the priests in charge of ceremonies.

All the major deities of the Incas were worshipped in the same temples, each with its own shrine. The shrines of the major deities—the Sun, Viracocha, the Thunder, and so on—had attendants; the more important the shrine, the more attendants were present. Different attendants had different functions: for example, some were in charge of divination, others of sacrifices, still others of day-to-day activities. The temples of the official Inca cult had their own group of consecrated women, the *mamaconas,* who were selected from the Chosen Women. These women did the same tasks as other Chosen Women, making chicha and textiles for the temples, but could not marry or be given as wives to officials. A woman of highest nobility was in charge of them. It is apparent that the mamacona for a temple served all the different deities at that temple; they were not exclusively for the use of the Sun.

In addition to the shrines of the Inca cult, there were many local shrines usually associated with particular huacas (discussed earlier). These might or might not have a temple or even a building, but most usually had some kind of attendant. Rowe (1946: 299) says that this attendant was typically an elderly man who could not help with other tasks. The shrines were not supported by the Inca agricultural tax but, rather, by the individuals for whom the place was sacred.

In addition to the religious specialists who officiated at the Inca cults and huacas, there were curers and sorcerors. *Curers* were individuals who claimed to have been contacted by spirits and told how to heal illnesses. *Sorcerors* were individuals who claimed to be able to speak with spirits and so were consulted when a person needed information, such as where a lost object could be found or what was happening far away. Sorcerors lived among the local people and were greatly feared (Rowe 1946: 302–303).

Particularly powerful sorcerors near Cuzco used small braziers of fire to speak with spirits. According to Rowe, they used ventriloquism to make it seem as if the fires were speaking to the person. These individuals were consulted only for the most serious matters and were paid well for their services.

RITUALS

To the Incas, the ritual, or practice of religious beliefs, was an essential aspect of life. One conducted rituals to ensure that one's life and well-being were not jeopardized, or to ward off evil spirits. If rituals were conducted properly, misfortunes could be avoided.

Almost all rituals were accompanied by some kind of sacrifice, most often guinea pigs or llamas but occasionally chil- **Sacrifices** dren. Most huacas were given llamas or guinea pigs. The main deities—Viracocha, the Creator; Inti, the Sun; and Illapa, the Thunder—always had distinctive colored llamas sacrificed to them: brown to Viracocha, white to Inti, and mixed color to Illapa. The animal was sacrificed by having its throat cut. Food, chicha, and coca were also given to huacas as sacrifices. The food and coca were usually burned, whereas the chicha was poured on the ground (Rowe 1946: 306–307). Cumbi cloth was also an important sacrificial item, especially to the Sun. Seashells, gold, silver, and corn flour were used as offerings as well.

The most important ceremonies, natural catastrophes, war, and the coronation of new kings involved sacrifices of humans—always children between the ages of 10 and 15. The children, always non-Incas, had to be physically perfect. The procedure involved a feast for the child so he or she would not go to Viracocha hungry. Following the feast the child would be strangled, its throat cut, or its heart cut out and offered to the deity still beating (Rowe 1946: 306). Sometimes children were sacrificed to mountain huacas by bringing them to the summit, getting them drunk, and then killing them (Reinhard 1992: 99–101).

The practice of child sacrifice might appear cruel to the reader, but one must remember that the sacrifice only occurred for the most important religious reasons. Humans were sacrificed for these events because they were considered the most worthy thing that could be offered to the gods. Children, rather than adults, were offered presumably because they were more pure in spirit than adults. Although it was no doubt a painful emotional experience for the families of the sacrificed children, to be selected was considered a great honor by both the child and his or her family.

Public Ceremonies
Numerous public ceremonies were associated with the calendars and with special events. Some ceremonies were held on a daily basis, such as the sacrifice of wood, food, and cloth to Inti. More elaborate ceremonies—including making sacrifices, dancing, feasting, and perhaps recounting important historical events—were held during times of crisis, at the coronation or death of a king, and during the various months of the calendar.

The three most important ceremonial months were *Capac Raymi* (December), *Aymoray* (May), and *Inti Raymi* (June). Bernabé Cobo (1990) offers detailed descriptions of these and other ceremonies. Capac Raymi celebrated the beginning of the rainy season and included the summer solstice, marking the longest day of the year. The most important rituals conducted were the male puberty rites (described in Chapter 3, Private Life and Culture). Ceremonies to other deities, especially Inti, were also conducted during this month. To emphasize the importance of the rituals, all non-Inca residents of Cuzco had to leave the center of town for the three weeks of the rites. They stayed in special areas near the main roads leading to their place of origin. When they returned at the end of the ceremony, they were fed lumps of corn flour mixed with the blood of sacrificed llamas. The lumps were said to be gifts from Inti to them, but ones that would inform the deity if the person spoke badly of it or the king. Several days of dancing and drinking chicha followed the return of the provincial residents of Cuzco, and the month closed with a special sacrifice on the last day. To celebrate the end of the puberty rites, and therefore the entrance into manhood of a new group of boys, food tribute from the provinces was delivered to Cuzco at this time (Rowe 1946: 309).

Aymoray took place in the modern month of May, to celebrate the corn harvest. People brought the corn from the fields, dancing and singing songs that asked that the corn not run out before the next harvest. Still singing and dancing, the people joined together in the city, where a large number of llamas were sacrificed. The raw meat from the llamas was distributed to all Incas, young and old, who ate some of it with toasted corn. Thirty other llamas were sacrificed and the meat burned at all the huacas in Cuzco, the most important ones receiving more meat, the less important ones receiving less meat.

Later in the month, more offerings of llamas were made to Inti in thanks for the corn harvest. Then the people assembled in a sacred field near Cuzco, where the boys who had received their emblems of manhood in the previous initiation ceremonies brought small sacks of the field's harvest into the city. Then everyone returned and plowed the field as a symbol of the importance of the corn harvest. Rituals to the corn deity, *mamazara*, were also conducted in each family's home to ensure an adequate supply of this grain.

Inti Raymi, celebrated in June, was the most important festival for the Sun god, Inti. The entire festival was conducted on a hill near Cuzco called Manturcalla, and only Inca males of royal blood were allowed to attend. On the first day 100 brown llamas were sacrificed. On the following days more llamas were sacrificed, not only to Inti but also to Viracocha and Illapa. Many statues were carved of wood, dressed in fine cumbi cloth, and burned at the end of the festival. A special dance was performed four times a day, with much drinking of chicha. After the sacrifices were made on Manturcalla, half the participants went to nearby hills to make further sacrifices while the rest stayed and danced. Llama figurines of gold, silver, and seashells were buried on the three nearby hills. The climax of the festival involved the sacrifice of special young llamas to Viracocha, whose image had been brought to Manturcalla on litters carried by important individuals. After this, all the charcoal and burned bones from the sacrifices were collected and deposited in a place near the hill, and everyone returned to Cuzco to continue singing and dancing for the rest of the day.

Every other month had associated rituals as well, making a full calendar of ceremonial events (see Chapter 4, Science and the Calendar). In addition, there were public ceremonies for special events such as war or natural catastrophe. Although the event might vary, the ceremony was the same. As with the initiation rites, all non-noble residents were sent away from Cuzco and all residents avoided eating salt, chili peppers, and chicha and refrained from sexual activity. The images of Viracocha, Inti, and Illapa were brought into the main square, along with the kings' mummies (which were also gods), and sacrifices—including children— were performed. Then boys under 20 years of age put on special costumes and walked around the square eight times, followed by a nobleman who scattered coca on the ground. The boys spent the night in the square praying to Viracocha and the Sun to end the particular problem that warranted the ceremony. In the morning, everyone broke their fast with a great feast and much chicha drinking, which lasted two days (Rowe 1946: 311).

Other Ceremonies   In addition to the ceremonies conducted according to the calendar and for the good of the empire, there were ceremonies for other purposes. These fall into three general categories: divination, curing, and sorcery. *Divination* is the attempt to foretell events in the future. This was widely practiced by the Incas, who rarely did anything without trying to divine the outcome. *Oracles* were supernatural figures that could answer questions about the future. They were the most powerful form of divination and were consulted only for important reasons, such as when to attack an enemy or if disease had struck a king. They might be human images or other figures. The Oracle of Pachacamac on the central coast south of Lima was described by Cobo as a wooden image carved into a "fierce and frightening figure." An important oracle near Cuzco was a post decorated with a golden band to which two golden breasts were attached. It was dressed in fine women's clothing, with a row of smaller figures on each side (Cobo 1990: 108).

An individual would approach the oracle and ask it a question. The oracle was said to answer in a voice that could be understood only by the priests or attendants of the oracle. There were four main oracles: the one near Cuzco, two on the coast near modern-day Lima, and one in the central highlands. At least one of these, the Oracle of Pachacamac south of Lima, predated the Incas, having been founded during the Middle Horizon.

For less serious divinations, the priests sacrificed a llama, took out a lung, and blew into a vein. The markings on the vein as it was distended indicated to the priest if the outcome would be positive or negative. The same ceremony could be conducted with guinea pigs, although these were used for less important divinations. Even simpler forms involved counting whether a group of pebbles had an even or odd number; chewing coca, spitting the juice on the hand, and seeing how it ran down the fingers; observing the movement of spiders or snakes; and burning llama fat or coca leaves and inspecting the way the fire burned (Rowe 1946: 303–304). It is obvious that the priests in charge of interpreting these signs had a great deal of influence in deciding what the outcome should be.

Sorcerors also could be consulted to foretell the future by speaking to evil spirits. Often they did this by drinking themselves into a stupor, which allowed them to see and speak to the spirits. This kind of divination was used by individuals for personal reasons. Sorcery was performed for the purpose of bringing misfortune or even death on another person. This was often done in a manner akin to modern voodoo, by making a figure of the person and piercing it with sharp objects or burning it. Another means was to obtain some part of the victim—such as hair, nails, skin, or teeth—and injure or harm it as a means of passing on that treatment to the victim. Sorcery was forbidden. Not only would a sorceror be put to death if discovered, but his entire family as well.

Unusual events could be interpreted as omens of good or evil, usually the latter. Eclipses and shooting stars were considered particularly bad luck. Rainbows, the hooting of an owl, or the howling of a dog were also signs of bad things to come. Dreams were important portents of good or evil, although the individual who had the dream interpreted its significance; there were no special interpreters of dreams.

Curing was another ceremony conducted by individuals. The Incas did not believe in natural causes of illness; all disease was thought to be caused by supernatural elements. Thus to get rid of a disease, one had to appease the spirit that was causing the illness. This usually involved some form of sacrifice to the offended spirit or huaca. Curers specialized in this activity, having been called to the occupation by spirits. The spirit gave the curer the power and knowledge of healing.

Curing involved a variety of other activities besides sacrifices. Many different plants were considered to have healing powers. In fact, some of these herbs have been tested for modern uses, and research is presently being conducted to determine whether any have commercial value.

The rituals involved with curing depended on what the cause of the disease was thought to be. If the illness was thought to be due to a failure to provide proper rituals for a huaca, then such was prescribed along with blowing the powder of corn and seashells toward the huaca. If the disease was thought to be caused by a foreign object in the person's body, the curer might simply massage the patient and suck on parts of the body where the pain was occurring. Usually the curer would produce an object that he claimed was the cause of the disease, such as a sharp object or some plant or animal material (Rowe 1946: 313). If the disease was identified as sorcery-induced, then a sorceror was needed to cure the patient. This might or might not be the same person, as there was no clear division between curing and sorcery.

Both Cobo and Guaman Poma mention very elaborate cures that were attempted for particularly grave illnesses. A small room was cleaned out completely; next the walls and floor were scrubbed with black corn powder, which was then burned in it; then the procedure was repeated with white corn powder. After the room was thus purified, the patient was brought in and laid on his or her back in the middle of the room. He or she was then put to sleep or into a trance, possibly through hypnotism. The curer pretended to cut the patient open and produced exotic objects, such as toads and snakes, which were burned as the causes of the illness.

An interesting Inca medical practice, which was known to earlier Andean societies as well, is *trepanation,* or cutting open the skull to expose the brain. This was no doubt done to let evil spirits out, but it had the added factor of danger that comes with working on the nerve center of the body. It is a credit to the Inca curers that many of these operations were successful, because many excavated skulls show evidence of having healed prior to death. In other examples there are multiple holes, indicating that the operation was performed more than once. It seems likely that the patient was in a drunken or drug-induced stupor, because the operation would have been very painful.

In contrast to the priests and priestesses in service to the official Inca religious shrines, both curers and sorcerors were parttime practitioners, doing the supernatural work in addition to their other jobs such as farming or making pottery.

6

Daily Life in the Inca Empire: Two Reconstructions

Many of the small details of life in the Inca empire—when ancient Andean people got up in the morning, or went to bed, or visited shrines—are not known with any accuracy. However, a possible daily routine can be reconstructed on the basis of (1) the few references in Spanish documents, and (2) the descriptions of contemporary groups who live a simple agricultural life that appears similar to the ancient people's. One drawback to using the latter is that such groups today have no obligatory state labor obligations, as did subjects of the Inca empire. In addition, nothing approximating the way of life of the Inca nobility exists today, making a reconstruction of a noble family's daily routine more hypothetical. The following reconstruction is for a family that is not royal—that is, not descended from the king or any previous king—but is nonetheless a member of the original Inca people from the Cuzco area.

A DAY IN THE LIFE OF AN INCA FAMILY IN CUZCO

The day begins around sunrise with the principal wife rising from bed, leaving her husband and 14-year-old son to sleep and going to awaken the secondary wife at her adjacent house. The latter dresses and leaves to get water from the river, waking her 12-year-old daughter to accompany her. They leave their one-room house in the family's compound, cross the courtyard, and exit through the narrow, trapezoidal doorway into the street. They turn and walk down the street toward the river, pausing to talk with a friend from the next house who is already returning. It is a happy coincidence that this friend is from the same group that the secondary wife is from, although from a different village. At least they speak the same native language. The secondary wife wishes the Incas did not forbid them to use it. It is amazing that they were both brought the month's walk to Cuzco from their native lands and ended up being neighbors!

Upon arriving at the river, she fills the one small and two large vessels she has brought with her, giving the smaller vessel to her daughter to carry. They return to the house, where the principal wife has stoked the fire from the embers of the previous night. The secondary wife begins preparing a meal of corn cooked with chili peppers under the watchful eye of the principal wife, who thinks to herself that this foreigner does not know the proper means for preparing food despite her training at the Inca center in her native land. Still, it is an honor for her husband to have been given this girl as a wife by the king in appreciation for his hard work for the empire. And she certainly makes life much easier.

Meanwhile, the husband and son have arisen and have begun discussing the day's activities. Breakfast is served on silver plates placed on a fine cloth on the floor. The principal wife sits with her back to her husband, facing the small clay stove where the food simmers. The secondary wife sits to her side, with her daughter next to her. The son sits next to his father. Everyone eats with spoons of silver.

After the meal the secondary wife cleans the dishes and places them back in a niche in the wall. She and her daughter then leave to collect firewood, taking some toasted maize with them, because they expect to be gone for several hours. Both take their spinning tools and wool from the family's alpacas to make thread on their way to the fields. They go to look for wood in the hills to the east of the city, the closest place where public land for such purposes can be found.

The husband leaves to visit the family fields near Cuzco and speak with the servants who work the fields. The irrigation canal bringing water to the fields is in need of repair, and he must discuss what is required to repair it before damage is done to the corn crop. He too takes a portion of toasted maize with him, along with his usual bag of coca and lime. The son leaves the cancha to visit cousins in the next one up the street, to discuss the upcoming puberty rites. They plan to go out to the fields and practice running for the race down the Hill of Anahuarque, which will be part of their rite of passage into manhood. They also plan to check the family's alpaca herd in the pastures above the city.

The principal wife remains at home and works on preparing the costume her son will wear during the puberty rites. She carefully sews a new tunic, adding some gold disks to the top where they will catch the sun as he dances in the ceremonies. She also visits with her husband's brother's wife, who lives in the house across the courtyard from theirs in the cancha. They have become good friends since the brother's wife's arrival several years earlier, even though she is six years younger than the principal wife. They have a second child on the way, their first having died two years ago. Both families suspect that the child died of sorcery, and they think it might have been caused by a neighbor jealous of the child. The principal wife stops abruptly—could the secondary wife have used a sorceror to do it?

After midday, the two go to leave an offering at the Temple of the Moon, to improve the prospects of a successful childbirth. The priestess there seems confident that the offering of a guinea pig and wool from a white llama will ensure a successful outcome this time. On their way home they speak to the maker of pots to arrange for some new cooking vessels to be delivered to their houses, because two got broken the day before. They pass by the cancha of the king's family, with its beautifully fitted stonework. How nice it would be to live in such a house, they say to each other. And to have so many yanaconas to do their bidding would be even better! Friends say the king's new country estate in the Uru-bamba valley is even more attractive, and that hundreds of conquered people were brought in from all over the empire to build it. The two women comment that although their lives are comparatively easy, how much easier seem the lives of the direct descendants of the Sun!

Returning home, they begin preparing the afternoon meal for their respective families. Slightly later, the secondary wife returns with the firewood. Told to prepare some more chicha for the festival coming up in three days, she goes to soak some corn in preparation. The principal wife prepares a stew of llama, potatoes, and quinoa for dinner, with corn dumplings on the side. Chicha is served in wooden goblets.

After dinner the secondary wife cleans up and puts the dinnerware away while the principal wife talks with her husband and son about their day. Before sunset the husband goes to speak with his brother about their alpaca herds, which the son found had strayed away from their pasture. The brother agrees to bring the herd back in the morning, and the son says he will go along to help. The father has to return to the fields to coordinate the repair of the irrigation canal, along with several other relatives who all have fields along the same irrigation system. The principal wife prepares offerings to the deities of the water and earth, to ensure everything will go well. After sunset the families return to their respective houses and go to bed, each family sharing a bed covered by alpaca cloaks for warmth against the cool night air.

A DAY IN THE LIFE OF A CONQUERED FAMILY

As the sun begins to rise in the Colca valley, located in Cuntisuyu to the west and south of Cuzco, a family of four slowly awakens. The mother gets up first and lights the fire, sending her oldest daughter, a

14-year-old, to get some more firewood from the ravine nearby. The girl leaves the house and runs past the other three houses nearby, through the fields to the ravine. She gathers some sticks and branches from the small bushes and trees and quickly returns home, greeting her cousin who is heading out to do the same.

Today is a day of excitement for the family, as the husband and father is returning from his service to the Incas, where he has been working as a laborer carrying tribute payments of quinoa to the Inca storehouses in the next valley. In addition, today might be the day the Inca official comes to select the girls to become Chosen Women, the hated position that takes young girls away, seldom to be seen again. Three years earlier the mother's niece was selected, and her family is still grieving. Although the Incas say she is being treated well, they have heard rumors of what happens to the girls: mistreated, forced to marry men who beat them, sometimes sacrificed to the hated Inca gods, taken far away from the only homes they know. The mother and father have been tempted to send their daughter away for the day, hoping the official will simply forget about her. Yet they know that the official's quipu keeps track of everything, from people to corn to cloth, and that she would be missed. The punishments for this are severe: death for disobeying the Inca king. It isn't worth the risk.

The youngest daughter sleeps fitfully in her wooden crib by the fire. She is only 2 years old and still has the flat boards strapped to her head that will mold her skull to the pleasing shape her society prefers. After the child's birth, the parents had gained new respect for the Moon Goddess, introduced by the Incas, for they had almost given up on having another child. The 18-year-old son is also sleeping, as he came home late the previous evening from his trip to distant fields. The trip took longer than usual because some of the individuals who went were still young men, unaccustomed to the harvest work done without an elder family member with them. So the work went slower, and they left later than expected. Also, one of the llamas became lame, and they stopped to kill and butcher it. Although the mother is glad it was not one of their llamas, as they had few enough since the Incas had taken so many, she muses that the meat would have been welcome.

While the food is cooking the daughter returns with the firewood. The mother wakes her son and they all eat together, sitting on the floor facing each other. They discuss what each will be doing and how good it will be to see their father and husband again. No one speaks of the other event of the day, for to speak of it might make it come true. After the meal, the daughter cleans the simple pottery bowls and spoons with which they eat all their meals. The mother nurses the younger daughter while the son repairs a net for catching birds and reattaches the stone tip of the footplow that he will be using later in the fields to harvest potatoes. He is glad his father will be home today to help him, as the additional work has made him extra tired over the past weeks.

As the sun rises slightly higher, the family leaves for the potato fields above the valley, accompanying some of their kinsmen and kinswomen. As they walk, the son thinks about the advantages of the new irrigation system they have built under Inca supervision: many more baskets of potatoes and quinoa are being grown than previously. What a shame they have to give so much to the Incas! And the fields are much closer to their homes than before, being located on the lower slopes of the hills rather than the upper parts. Even the small part of the old field system that has been reconstructed to use an irrigation channel is yielding many bushels of crops, justifying the effort made. He is still not sure the large reservoir on the top of the hill will end up being worth the effort, but if there are serious droughts it might well make the difference between a harvest and nothing. However, there have not been many droughts recently—certainly nothing like the stories the old people tell of the past, when there were many years of no rainfall.

As the mother and daughter walk along, they do some spinning of wool. The mother thinks of other work she still has to do: weaving some clothes for her son. The mother knows her husband will not need any new clothes for a time, because the Incas provide them at the center. Thank the gods for that! Yet she also knows her husband will have to make himself some new sandals, as his old ones will be completely worn out by the traveling between field and storehouse. Her young daughter cries softly so she nurses her, not stopping to rest. After the child finishes she gives her to the other daughter to carry for a while. She hopes fervently to be able to see grandchildren from her!

The agricultural work is long and hard, for they have to farm the Incas' fields as well as their own. A new section of terraces had to be built last year to satisfy the Incas' demands for quinoa. Constructing the retaining walls for the terraces is always difficult, made more so by the presence of the Inca supervisor and his arrogant attitude. These terraces were especially difficult because they are on a steeper slope, and more soil had to be collected to fill them in. But she knows that once built, the terraces will outlive her and probably even her children.

The workers harvest the quinoa for several hours, then pause to eat their toasted maize and flat bread. They take more coca and lime, to make the work less painful, and work until the sun is low over the western mountains. Then the group packs up the baskets on their llamas and heads down to the village.

On the way home the mother stops at the small shrine of her personal deity and leaves a special offering of a guinea pig in hopes that the deity will make the Inca official choose someone else's daughter. But what a prayer to be making! Asking for someone else's child to be taken from them forever—perhaps another relative's! Why do they need so many children? Why so many from their village, it seems? Then she remembers what her husband told her, after talking to men from other villages. The same story is told everywhere.

Maybe they should rebel and simply refuse to send their children or their tribute. But then she also remembers the stories the men told of other villages that had done this, and how the Incas had come again and killed their leaders and moved the entire village away, who knows where! The people who came to replace them were from somewhere far away, far enough that they spoke a different language, difficult to understand. And such strange clothes they wore!

When the family arrives at home they are relieved to see their husband and father setting out his things from the trip. He arrived a while earlier, after a long walk. He says he heard the Inca official was not coming until the next day, which means that the selection will not take place until the following day. Two more days at least! The thought is a small comfort.

The family sits down to a meal of quinoa and potato stew, with a small portion of guinea pig in it as a special treat. They speak of what has happened during the husband's absence, how another section of irrigation canal has been completed and some new terraces begun. It has been less difficult to do this section, as it is lower than the earlier ones and the soil is less rocky. However, the work has been slow, as more men have been called up to fight in the army. The Incas have been starting campaigns to expand their rule to areas of jungle far to the north of the Colca valley, and they need additional warriors. The round trip to the war zone is long, making the service even longer. And this is in addition to the laborers working at other activities, as the husband has been doing. They are all glad he was not called for the war, and they hope that by the time it is their household's turn to send someone else for work, the war will be over. If not, their son will be a prime candidate for the war effort. As the evening turns colder the family wraps themselves in blankets of coarse llama wool and goes to bed, happy to be together again.

7

The Inca Contribution to Modern Andean Culture

THE CONQUEST OF THE INCAS AND ITS AFTERMATH

The high point of the Inca empire can be said to have occurred during the reign of Huayna Capac, which ended at his death in A.D. 1527. The empire had reached its maximum size, and the organizational changes implemented by Pachacuti and Topa Inca aimed at unifying the conquered ethnic groups were well on their way to being attained. Huayna Capac, Topa Inca's heir, reigned for 34 years but died suddenly without naming an heir of his own. His eldest son, Huascar, who lived in Cuzco, claimed the kingship. However, another son, Atahuallpa, who had lived with his father in Quito, was proclaimed king of Quito and an equal to Huascar. The two rivals gathered armies and began a civil war that tore the empire apart. Because of the better training and experience of Atahuallpa's armies and the superiority of his generals, he was victorious.

The Spanish explorer Pizarro landed on the northern coast of Peru in A.D. 1532. Atahuallpa was traveling south to Cuzco, to be invested as the Inca king after the defeat of Huascar. Through interpreters, Atahuallpa agreed to a meeting with the Spaniards near Cajamarca, a city in the northern Peruvian highlands. The Spaniards organized a surprise attack and captured Atahuallpa, holding him for ransom. Although the Incas gave them enough gold and silver to fill half a room, the Spaniards killed the Inca king, installed a puppet ruler in his place, and proceeded to Cuzco, where they took control of the empire.

The Inca empire had grown to its maximum size in less than a century. Yet between A.D. 1532 and 1534, it was conquered by Francisco Pizarro and 260 Spaniards. How was this possible? Two factors were clearly important. The first was the Inca civil war between Huascar and Atahuallpa that had ended just before the Spaniards' arrival. This war pitted Inca armies and royal ayllus against each other. After the final defeat of Huascar's armies, Atahuallpa's victorious generals rounded up and executed all the Inca nobility of Cuzco who had been loyal to Huascar. Thus the unity that had made the Incas such a military power was severely weakened before the Spaniards arrived.

The second factor was the rapid spread of European diseases throughout the Andean region. Atahuallpa's and Huascar's father, Huayna Capac, died suddenly—historians think it was probably from epidemic disease. These epidemics, such as measles, smallpox, typhus, and influenza, were brought to Mexico by the Spaniards in their conquests of that region starting in A.D. 1519. The diseases spread southward through the native peoples, ultimately reaching Peru. The native peoples of the New World had no resistance to these diseases and were ravaged by them. In some areas as much as 90 percent of the population died, leaving the survivors psychologically devastated (Bruhns 1994: 375). Because epidemics spread more rapidly in regions of high population density, coastal communities were reduced more than highland ones. This dramatic loss by disease probably did more than the Spanish horses and guns to contribute to the Incas' conquest.

THE INCAS UNDER SPANISH RULE

It is impossible to fully understand the way of life of either the Incas or their conquered peoples because of the incomplete record, both historical and archaeological. Thus it is difficult to determine how much of the way of life that exists today owes its roots to Inca and pre-Inca cultures. Part of the difficulty also arises from the widespread changes introduced into native groups by the Spaniards after the conquest.

Many writers have discussed these changes (for a particularly good example, see George Kubler's [1946] *The Quechua in the Colonial World*). A fundamental point to understand about the Spanish Conquest is how utterly different the Spanish way of life was for the Andean people. When the Incas conquered most of western South America, they imposed a system that was rooted in a way of life generally similar to that of the conquered peoples. As has been noted repeatedly, the Incas tried to disrupt their subjects' way of life as little as possible. The Inca view of government was to act like a large-scale kin group, exacting tribute and labor in ways that were understood by conquered people from their own patterns of activities. People were allowed to keep parts of their own fields, grow their own crops, and worship their own gods. The Inca state was like a family to which one owed work and food, and which in turn provided services and security for oneself and one's family.

In contrast, the Spaniards imposed a way of life on the Andean people that was completely different economically, politically, socially, and religiously (Silverblatt 1987). Spain was a part of the emerging market economy of Europe, which was based on the marketplace forces of supply and demand and the importance of accumulating wealth. The Spanish Conquest itself was motivated by the desire to gain the enormous riches of the Inca empire, measured in gold and silver. This was the same currency that was used in Europe. Some of the most fundamental changes wrought in the Andean world had to do with the Spaniards' requirements for labor to work the gold and silver mines of Peru (which encompassed most of western South America as originally defined by the Spanish conquerors).

Even more fundamental was the difference in what could be called the worldview of the Spaniards. Their model of conqueror–conquered was one of domination and exploitation; to the victor belonged the spoils. Although official Spanish policy was to leave native culture alone except where it contradicted Spanish law, seldom was that practiced.

The time following the Spanish conquest of the Inca empire is divided into several distinct periods (Kubler 1946). During the first period, the Conquest Quechua Period (A.D. 1532–1572), the Spaniards consolidated their control over the Inca empire. It marked a critical time of transition when Spanish institutions were introduced, but the basic way of life remained largely unchanged for many Andean people away from direct Spanish contact. Kubler (1946: 341) notes that there were two distinct patterns of life during this period: pacified Quechua and separatist Quechua. Here the term *Quechua* is used to denote any native individual, Inca or non-Inca, who spoke the Quechua language. The pacified Quechuas were natives who accepted their conquest by the Spaniards and were incorporated into that way of life. The separatists were those who attempted to maintain the old Inca ways of doing things, rejecting and resisting Spanish influences. It is ironic that the separatists actually had to change their way of life much more, because they were essentially living an armed camp existence. Class differences were reduced, because everyone was involved in fighting. The economy was modified by the need to obtain Spanish material for resistance, especially horses and weapons. Finally, the separatist Quechuas were targeted for vigorous missionary activities by the Spaniards, which the natives curiously allowed. Thus their culture was changed to a large degree (Kubler 1946: 343–345).

In contrast, pacified Quechuas were subjected to much less direct pressure and influence. The amount of change in this group was directly proportional to the proximity of the natives to Spanish settlements. The closer they lived to the Spaniards, the more they changed—both voluntarily and involuntarily. Also affecting the transformation of Inca culture were the ways in which the classes in Inca society were assimilated into the colonial structure. The Spaniards adopted the Inca policy of using the curacas as foremen in their interactions with the native workers. Thus these former lower-level Inca bureaucrats became lower-level Spanish ones and quickly were assimilated into the Spanish way of life. In contrast, the workers maintained much of their previous way of life, providing only those new goods required of them by the Spaniards. In addition, the Inca m'ita was continued and the work provided was used for maintaining public works, much as it had been for the Incas.

Although one might expect that the Spanish Conquest reduced the class differences between the Incas and their conquered peoples, in fact it did not. The Spaniards granted the upper nobility of Inca society—including all of the Inca class and the non-Inca curacas of the provinces—status as landowners. This was denied to the labor class of the Inca empire, the conquered people who were not curacas (Silverblatt 1987: 112). The distinction allowed the former to own land and denied that right to the latter. More important, however, it made the Inca and non-Inca nobility exempt from tribute payments and labor demands. As a result, the upper class of Inca society participated in the accumulation of land at the expense of their own people. In this way the upper classes were assimilated into Spanish colonial society as approximate equals with the Spaniards, whereas the lower class was designated socially inferior. What also added to this was intermarriage of Spaniards and Incas, especially Spanish men with Inca women of high class.

Contributing to the transformation of the Inca culture into a Spanish colonial one was the Spanish policy of *encomienda*. This was a grant of native labor given by the Spanish Crown to the Spaniards as a reward for their part in the conquest of the Incas. The award did not give the land itself to the Spaniards, only the rights to use the indigenous people's labor to produce goods. There was a hitch, however: if the natives could not meet the tribute requirements of their *encomendero* (the person who had control over the encomienda grant), then their lands could be put up for sale to recover the lost payments. It simply became the practice to raise tribute costs to a level so high that the local people could not pay them and had to sell their land to the Spaniards. Thus the loss of native lands to the conquerors began during the first years after the Spanish Conquest.

The encomienda system had two other results besides the loss of native lands. The first was the introduction of European crops and animals to the indigenous population of Peru. However, most of these crops and animals were raised solely for tribute. The local people continued to grow their own Andean food for consumption. The second result was the increase in landless people as a consequence of the sale of their lands through foreclosure. As more and more land was bought by the Spaniards, more and more people abandoned their land and went to work as Spanish servants (Kubler 1946: 341–343).

The Conquest Quechua Period is also marked by rebellions, especially during the first years of the conquest. The most serious was the 1536 rebellion led by Manco Inca (an Inca noble who was a protégé of Pizarro) that nearly overthrew Spanish rule. In A.D. 1535, Manco Inca realized that the changes brought by the Spaniards were doing great harm to the Inca people, so he organized a massive effort to throw off the Spanish rule. He secretly organized resistance that would attack the Spanish simultaneously in several areas.

On April 18, 1536, an Inca army estimated to number about 180,000 men laid siege to Cuzco (where only 190 Spaniards lived), supported by several hundred loyal natives. The Spaniards, although greatly outnumbered, had the advantage of occupying the center of Cuzco; its narrow streets only allowed small numbers of men to attack any given area. This also increased the effectiveness of the Spanish horsemen. The Incas countered this advantage by burning the thatch roofs of the houses and attacking along the rooflines. After a week of attacks and counterattacks the Incas appeared close to crushing the Spaniards, but a desperate counterattack by the Spanish horsemen drove them back. This allowed the Spaniards to gain control of the old fortress of Sacsahuaman, and from there they progressively beat back the Incas until the siege finally broke down completely in the spring of 1537, 18 months after it began.

While the Incas were attacking Cuzco, another army laid siege to Lima. This siege lasted only 12 days but came close to driving the Spaniards back onto their ships (Kubler 1946: 383). But with the relatively rapid securing of Lima the rebellion in the rest of Peru never gained hold, and Spanish control over the Incas was restored.

During the next historical period, the Early Colonial Period (A.D. 1572–1650), native life continued to be transformed. The period began with the imposition of the policy of *reducción,* or reduction, by the administrator of Peru, Viceroy Toledo. Under this policy, indigenous people were moved away from their native communities among the fields and were settled in new towns of Spanish design. The pattern of towns seen in the Andes today, of streets running at 90-degree angles with a central plaza where the main cathedral is located, is a product of this policy. The purpose was to improve the collection of tribute and labor payments, and to increase the process of converting the local people to Christianity. It effectively lumped mem-

Early Colonial Period (A.D. 1572–1650)

bers of different ayllus together and made the farming of former fields impractical by increasing the travel time to them. This broke up the peoples' ancient sense of ownership of the land and led to conflicts over land use. Moreover, because potential marriage partners from one's own ayllu might have been moved to distant towns, members of different ayllus began to marry, which violated the pre-Inca tradition of marrying within one's ayllu. Both factors had the effect of further breaking up indigenous cultural practices.

In addition to the reduction, during this period the conversion of the native economy from Andean crops to introduced European ones progressed. The Spaniards could require virtually anything of their encomienda workers, and they were much more interested in their own kinds of foods than local ones. Consequently, typical Spanish plants (e.g., wheat, barley, dates, and olives) and animals (e.g., sheep, cattle, pigs, and chickens) began to be grown and bred by the natives. However, most of these had little impact on the natives' diet; they continued to eat only their own food. This led to a split in the natives' economic activities, because some foods had to be grown for tribute and others for their own consumption. As tribute requirements became heavier, progressively fewer native foods could be grown by the encomienda workers.

Whether an introduced plant or animal was adopted into the native economy depended on several factors, such as its adaptability to different zones, its ability to compete with native foods, its new uses, and whether it involved excessive amounts of additional labor or resources, either land or irrigation (Kubler 1946: 355–357). Some European foods, such as sugarcane and cattle, became very popular among Andean people—the former because it provided a sweet, the latter because of its adaptability and many uses. Thus despite the Incas' predilection for their own foods, the native economy was transformed from a strictly Andean one to a mixed one through the cultivation of European crops and farm animals.

The practice of granting encomiendas to Spaniards dropped off dramatically during the seventeenth century. These grants were only for a specified period of time; once the time had lapsed, the land and the people on it reverted to the use of the Spanish Crown. This is one reason why the encomenderos were so anxious to find means to buy land. However, as a result of the abuses of the encomienda system, the Spanish Crown replaced it with the *corregimiento* system, which placed a Spanish government official, called a *corregidor*, in charge of the lands and people of a former encomienda. This saved the native lands from being sold, thereby preserving the property rights of many groups. But the members of the corregimiento had to provide labor to the corregidor, much like the Inca m'ita system. This provided the Spanish administration with a huge pool of labor, which was put to use in the government's gold and silver mines (Kubler 1946: 346). Thousands of Andean men perished

working in the ghastly conditions of the mines. This led to further abandonment of native lands, as people fled the required work in the mines.
In addition, the corregidors were paid not by the government but out of
the products of their corregimiento. Consequently they began to abuse
their power in much the same way as the encomenderos had. Life continued to be grim for local people, despite the good efforts at reform on
the part of the Spanish government.

Another transformation was occurring during the late sixteenth and
early seventeenth centuries: the conversion of indigenous people to
Christianity. Christianity dictated that the world was divided into good
and evil: those that worshipped the God of the Bible, and those who did
not. Christianity provided the moral grounds for the conquest of the Inca
empire, for it was seen as full of devil worship. Because of the political
turmoil following the Spanish Conquest and the relative lack of priests
in Peru, very little conversion was attempted or achieved during the first
40 years of the colonial era. After that time, however, more effort was
put into the so-called *extirpation of idolatry*, or stamping out of native
religious practices. Priests made a concerted effort both to convince local
people of the superiority of the Spanish faith and to actively persecute
individuals practicing native forms of worship. During this time many
of the ancestor mummies of local ayllus were searched out and burned,
and the Inca priests and priestesses punished.

Paradoxically, as the attack on native religion increased, the importance of women in preserving the indigenous practice also increased
(Silverblatt 1987: Ch. 5). As men's role in the political and social life of
the colonial era increased, they became too public to be involved in the
secret practice of ancient religious rituals. Therefore the important roles
fell to women (formerly restricted to being attendants in the Inca religion), who moved the locus of such activities away from the towns and
villages to caves in the high puna area. Here, far from the prying eyes
of Spanish priests and officials, the ancient religious beliefs associated
with ancestor and huaca worship continued. The strong role that such
practices continue to have in the religion of many farmers in isolated
villages today (Allen 1988) is a tribute to the ability of the colonial
women to preserve these beliefs, as well as to the power of the beliefs
themselves.

The corregimiento system, the Catholic missionary work, the reduction, and the intensified mining led to a general increase in the movement of native people away from their homes during this period. Some
people moved into the eastern lowlands, where Spanish influence was
not as marked. Others simply gave up their lands, or were forced off of
them, and became servants of both the Spaniards and the growing lower
class of native curacas in service to the Spaniards. More of the economy
was being driven by the need for goods for markets, rather than for the

Inca sorcerors represented as devils. *Top*,
sorceror of dreams; *middle*, sorceror of fire;
bottom, sorceror healing an individual by
sucking out illness.

needs of the natives. Thus the basic Andean way of life continued to
change. Although many aspects of life remained similar, such as the
agricultural practices, the Inca way of life no longer existed; it had become a Spanish colonial one.

Other changes occurred during the subsequent 300 years, including a
series of rebellions in the 1700s (all unsuccessful), the Wars of Indepen-
dence from Spain in the 1800s (all successful), and the gradual development of modern, technologically oriented societies in the twentieth
century. When one looks at modern Lima, with its buses and modern
buildings, its hustle and bustle, it is hard to imagine anything of the Inca
way of life is left. And in cities like Lima, very little is. But one does not
have to travel far out of any city in Peru, Ecuador, or Bolivia to reach
areas where the Inca presence is still evident, especially in the highlands.

A woman in the traditional dress of the Colca valley. Note her son's western dress.

The farther from modern civilization one goes, the closer one gets to a way of life that is much like the one described in the previous chapters.

There is a marked contrast in modern Peru between coastal and highland societies. The coastal towns are much more closely tied to the national economy, which in turn is a part of the world economy. Market forces of supply and demand control people's lives, and most farming is for profit, not subsistence. Towns are still laid out on the ancient reduction pattern, but they are modern in style. Concrete is a major construction material, but adobe is used frequently owing to its lower cost. Modern conveniences of electricity and plumbing are present, as are paved roads and sidewalks. People wear western clothes, such as jeans and t-shirts. Businessmen and businesswomen wear suits. People speak Spanish and even a second language, such as English. Catholicism is the main religion, although modern Protestant religions are becoming more popular.

In contrast, highland society is much more diverse. Life in the major cities and towns is very much like life in the coastal centers, although it is not uncommon to see people dressed in nonwestern clothes: a poncho, or a colorfully embroidered dress with a felt hat. Most people have jobs that pay a wage, but in some towns (e.g., the Department of Ancash's capital of Huaraz) many people still own fields and farm them for their own use. Although Spanish is the language most often heard, it is possible to hear Quechua or Aymara (the indigenous language of the Lake Titicaca region) spoken in the streets and marketplaces.

Some communities, far removed from the major highways and towns that have brought western civilization to the Andes, remain very much like the villages described by the earliest chroniclers. For example, Sonqo is a dispersed settlement of farmers to the east of Cuzco who live among their fields, belong to ayllus, and speak Quechua, although most individuals know Spanish as well. Catholicism is mixed with ancient religious beliefs, such as divination and powerful mountain deities (Allen 1988).

INCA CONTRIBUTIONS TO MODERN
ANDEAN SOCIETY

The Inca, and pre-Inca, contributions to modern Andean culture can be discussed under the categories of agriculture, engineering, community organization, and religion.

Agriculture Probably the most enduring aspect of pre-Hispanic culture is the widespread use of native plants and animals. Corn, beans, squash, potatoes, quinoa, ullucu, coca, llamas, alpacas, and guinea pigs all are still used commonly, although much more so in highland communities. In fact, if the Spaniards had not required wheat, barley, rice, grapes, apples, peaches, cattle, sheep, and other common foods to be used as tribute payments, Spanish foods might be little used today.

One of the Incas' greatest contributions to modern agriculture was the development of large, irrigated terrace systems for growing crops. Studies in the Colca valley of southern Peru have indicated that virtually all the agriculture today is practiced on field systems built or expanded by the Incas (Malpass 1987). Similar studies in other regions suggest likewise. The Incas were expert farmers who learned how to most effectively utilize local regions for agricultural purposes. That their systems are still serving today's inhabitants is a testimony to their skills.

Engineering In addition to the agricultural systems, which reflect engineering skills as well as agricultural ones, other aspects of Inca engineering remain in modern Andean culture. Many examples of Inca buildings still exist and are still used, despite over 400 years of earthquakes and other seismic disturbances. The foundations of the Church of Santo Domingo in Cuzco consist of the original Coricancha, the interior design of which was exposed in this century by

Inca stone foundation for a modern building in Cuzco.

an earthquake. Many other major buildings in Cuzco also have Inca foundations.

Inca bridges remained in use for centuries over some of the major rivers in the central Andes. One was still in use and drawn by the American traveler George Squier when he passed through Peru in the 1870s (Squier 1877). Although it is doubtful that any bridge was the original one dating to Inca times, many continued to be rebuilt and maintained by local villages in the same manner as they were under Inca rule.

Even though it may seem that all vestiges of the original Inca settlement patterns were eradicated by the reduction, there still exist villages dispersed among the fields that are suggested as being Inca or pre-Inca (Mishkin 1946: 439). This is perfectly reasonable, given that the reduction policy focused on the areas of greatest importance to the Spaniards. The basic house of a rural family in the Cuzco area today is also very similar to the original Inca ones, being rectangular with a single room and a gabled roof (Allen 1988: 68). As in Inca and pre-Inca times, families live close together, and it is not uncommon for newlyweds to live in the home of one of their parents for a while.

Community Organization
As the village pattern in some communities still reflects the Inca arrangement, so does the social organization. The ayllu is still a fundamental unit of Andean society outside the commercial centers. Even though the ayllu is not the same as it was before the Spanish Conquest, it retains many of its original functions of regulating land use and marriage patterns. Ayllus have pasture land and fields for members' use, along with irrigation systems where needed. Ayllu members work together in maintaining the irrigation systems.

Many communities still have the Hanansaya and Hurinsaya moiety divisions introduced by the Incas. In the Colca valley town of Coporaque, the two moieties participate yearly in the cleaning of the main water reservoir for their fields. The reservoir has an irrigation channel that divides it into two parts, and each moiety clears the plants and rubble from its half.

Kinship and property rights also follow pre-Hispanic patterns. Both men and women own property and pass it down to their offspring. The terms people use for their relatives are Quechua, not Spanish, concepts. Of course, the continued use of the Quechua language is an indication of the extent to which the Inca way of life continues in many areas.

Religion
Religion among Quechua-speaking people in the Andes is usually described as a combination of (1) Catholicism introduced by the Spaniards, and (2) pre-Hispanic beliefs; but it is difficult to determine what particular beliefs belong to which source. This is because the Catholic religion introduced by the Spaniards was not the pure religion practiced in the major cathedrals of Europe; rather, it was a mixture of Christian and pagan beliefs of Spain introduced by the Spanish conquerors who were not noble men of good education and faith. They were in large measure poor and illiterate men whose religious heritage was a specialized form of Christianity that accommodated supernatural beings and forces other than those of the Christian gods and saints. Thus the imposition of Catholicism accommodated local Andean beliefs, because the latter bore similarities to the conquistadors' own. From a modern perspective, however, this makes it exceedingly difficult to discern the Spanish influences from the Inca influences.

In addition, local Andean people learned during the great extirpation of idolatry in the seventeenth century to mask their own rituals and holiday celebrations within the Catholic ones. Spanish observances of Christmas, for example, fall around the Inca holiday of Capac Raymi (see Chapter 5, Religion); thus celebration of the one became a celebration of the other. One of the most sacred rituals today in the area of Cuzco is the trip to the mountain of Qoyllur Rit'i, done to celebrate the appearance of the Christ Child to a shepherd there in 1785. This takes place during the festival of Corpus Christi, one of the major Catholic holidays. The trip is made to visit the shrine at the place where the Christ Child appeared. Yet the holiday is much more important to local people as the time to visit the home of the spirits of the snow and mountains (Allen 1988: 190). The entire festival has many pre-Hispanic aspects.

Although the idea of God in present-day Andean religion is a result of Spanish influence, people believe that He is too powerful and distant to be interested in the affairs of humans. This perspective is similar to the beliefs concerning Viracocha, the god of creation. In fact, in some areas God and Jesus Christ are equated with the Sun, or Inti (Allen 1988: 52; Mishkin 1946: 463). Thus little worship or ritual is conducted specifically toward these figures, other than the Christian rites in the Catholic Church.

In the vicinity of Cuzco (and in other areas of the former empire as well), local spirits are much more important to modern rural people, the descendants of the Incas, because they are seen as having a more active interest in the lives of humans. These spirits are given different names in different areas but have in common the fact that their presence is tied to a particular place. This is the equivalent of the huacas of the Incas. Mountain huacas are especially powerful, as they were to the Incas, and there also is a hierarchy of spirits (Allen 1988: Ch. 1). There is a strong belief in the idea of Pacha-Mama, the Earth Mother, which is unquestionably ancient; her influence is likewise considered to be profound.

The places of the dead and their spirits are also considered important, and there is a connection between the ancient Inca burial structures (chullpas) and the spirits of those people (Allen 1988: 54–59). The spirits are considered to be dangerous to people but good for the potato harvest. Objects are also considered to have supernatural powers, much the same as for the Incas.

As with the Incas, modern Andean people have a strong belief in sorcery and divination, and sorcerors are feared. They use a variety of materials, but coca is central to all of them. Chicha is frequently used as well. Divination is done with coca leaves. Chicha and other alcoholic beverages are used as offerings to the spirits of places and to Pacha-Mama, both by sorcerors and commoners, following the pre-Hispanic pattern described by the first Spanish chroniclers.

In summary, it might be said that the way of life of rural Andean communities owes as much to its pre-Hispanic heritage as it does to its colonial one. Not only are many of the crops indigenous, but the field systems, agricultural techniques, social organization, and religious practices are as well. Although it is obvious that the Spaniards wrought significant changes in the Inca way of life, it is equally obvious that the pre-Hispanic way of life was resilient enough to maintain much of itself despite those changes.

What has been destroyed completely and utterly are the political institutions that defined the Inca empire. However, one could argue that the Inca way of life is still present (although in a highly modified form), mostly in the highlands. Andean ways of doing things persist; they have simply incorporated those aspects of European culture that were either useful or imposed. In many areas the people strongly identify themselves as the direct ancestors of the Incas, and they take pride in the accomplishments of their ancient relatives. It is a well-deserved pride.

ANDEAN CONTRIBUTIONS TO THE MODERN WORLD

The effect of the Andean region on the development of present-day societies has been enormous. Consider some of the foods originally grown in this region. Corn was domesticated in both the Andes and Mexico, and it has become one of the five most important food crops in the world. Another important crop is the potato, in the United States called the "Irish" potato. In fact, it was introduced to Ireland from Peru. Italian and Spanish food is based on the tomato, which was originally a South American plant. Peanuts, several varieties of beans, hot peppers, squash, pineapples, manioc, sweet potatoes, and cashews are from South America as well (Bruhns 1994: 378–380). Another crop that has had an enormous effect on virtually all cultures of the world—although not a positive one—is tobacco, which is also of South American origin.

Yet another result of the conquest of the Incas (and the Aztecs of Mexico) was widespread inflation in Europe, owing to the huge influx of gold and silver into Spain. But this money had positive effects as well, including financing much of the Renaissance artwork in Spain and other parts of Europe.

In an excellent summary of the impact of the European conquest of the Americas, Bruhns (1994: Ch. 19), notes that the development of slavery also was tied to the rise of commercial agriculture in the New World. Sugar was in great demand in Europe, so plantations for growing it were started in the Caribbean. Native Americans were used as the first slaves on these plantations; but as they quickly died off, Africans were brought over to do the work. As other crops were developed and mining increased, the need for more slaves intensified, leading to the importation of more and more Africans. Indeed, the ethnic and biological diversity of all the New World countries, from Canada to Argentina, owes much to this event.

In conclusion, the Incas had a profound impact on the world in which they lived, and much of that impact can be seen in Andean communities today. One cannot help but wonder how the history of world civilization might have been different had Atahuallpa not been captured by the Pizarro in A.D. 1532.

8

Epilog: Preserving the Past

The past is not seen from objects alone. Cultures are not just things in glass cases. They come with context and association, with dates and with provenance.

—Litvak King 1990: 206

The first chapter of this book discusses the question of how we know what happened in the past. We have three different sources of information about the Incas: historical records written by early Spaniards, archaeological research, and studies of modern people living in the Andes. Through these sources the outline of the Inca way of life is fairly clear, although many details remain unknown. How can more be learned about the Incas? Only by finding more documents in archives in Spain and South America, by locating and excavating more sites dating to the Inca period, and by doing more studies of modern farmers. Unfortunately, each of these possibilities has limitations.

Given the rapid transformation of modern Andean society, it is unlikely that much more can be learned about the Inca way of life from studying modern people. The lives of even the most remote farmers are being touched by the modern world. Radio, television, and modern roads are bringing rapid changes to all Andean people. Nonetheless, researchers study these isolated communities to learn how the people survive, and in this way they determine what kinds of ancient patterns still exist. Catherine Allen's 1988 study of Sonqo is a fine example of this.

It is also possible that more documents will be found as researchers examine archives in Spain and South America. Although many early documents were found in Spain, in more recent times the discoveries in local archives in Peru have been important. For example, sixteenth- and seventeenth-century reports of Spanish officials concerning the Colca valley, found in a church archive in Yanque, a small village in that valley, has provided a wealth of information about the original inhabitants of the valley and their relationships with people in surrounding regions (Pease 1977).

Unfortunately, the use of early Spanish documents has several drawbacks. Mainly, the Spanish descriptions are uneven, focusing in great detail on some things while ignoring others. Therefore, even though there is a wealth of information about the Inca way of life in Cuzco, there is much less about the way of life of (1) the Inca nobles in the provinces, or (2) the conquered people. Therefore, the use of the archaeological record to expand on the historical documents is essential.

The archaeological record is unique in certain respects. Whereas an old document can be reread many times and one can return and ask modern people questions again and again, archaeological sites cannot be re-excavated to find out more. Excavations, no matter how carefully done, destroy as they proceed. Once an area has been excavated, there is no way to get that piece of the past back; it is gone forever. Thus it is important that every piece of information be collected and saved, no matter how small or seemingly insignificant.

This is why archaeologists never excavate an entire site at one time. Only as much is excavated as is needed to find answers to researchers' questions. In this way, other people with other questions can return to the site later and still find areas to excavate for answers. It is important to leave part of every site unexcavated for another reason as well: new techniques of interpreting or dating sites are being discovered all the time, so it is useful to leave an area that could be assessed with newer techniques in the future. Consider the invention of radiocarbon dating, the principal means by which archaeologists assign calendar dates to sites. Prior to the late 1940s, when archaeologists dug up old fireplaces they simply threw the charcoal away, thinking it was useless. Then physicists discovered that charcoal could be used for dating the age of a site. Researchers could go back to many sites and find other fireplaces (because they had not excavated the entire sites), so many dates were obtained for these ancient cultures. If the sites had been completely dug, there would have been no way of going back and learning how old they were.

AN ARCHAEOLOGICAL PROBLEM

Unfortunately, many Inca and pre-Inca sites are being destroyed before archaeologists can excavate them. There are two main causes of this destruction. One is development, including the growth of towns and cities, as well as industrial activities. As the population of the Andean countries has grown, more and more houses, factories, and municipal buildings have been constructed, sometimes in the same locations as earlier Inca sites. Cuzco, the Inca capital, now has a population of several hundred thousand, which is ten or twenty times its size during Inca times. The remains of Inca Cuzco now lie buried under modern Cuzco or completely destroyed by its urban expansion. The only exceptions are the few Inca structures that were used as foundations for colonial buildings.

A second, and in many ways more serious, cause of Inca site destruction is looting or plundering. Looting has occurred since the early days of the Spanish Conquest, when the Europeans dug into anything that looked like it might contain Inca or pre-Inca treasures. In fact, the Huaca del Sol, the largest Moche pyramid in existence, was three-quarters destroyed when the Spaniards diverted the Moche River to undermine its foundation in order to find what treasure lay inside.

Today, however, Inca and pre-Inca sites are menaced not by large-scale operations but by small groups of individuals who work at night, digging in ancient settlements and cemeteries to find pots, gold, and silver to sell. These *huaqueros*, or looters, are looking for anything of value and do not care what means they use to obtain it. Sometimes they are even armed. The work of huaqueros can be seen at any site in Peru. Deep holes pockmark the ground, as if a close-packed group of bombs had struck the area. Bones, cloth, pottery fragments, and other materials are strewn about. Such wanton destruction is truly a sad sight.

The loss that huaqueros have caused to our understanding of the past is immeasurable; but to understand why looting is such a tragedy, one must understand how good archaeology is done. Archaeology is an exacting science. First, researchers must excavate a site very carefully, sometimes using tools as small as dental picks and toothbrushes to carefully remove the dirt from around a fragile pot, tool, or skeleton. Then the following information must be recorded for each fragment or object: where it was found, what was found near it, whether it was in a structure or out in the open, and so on. Drawings and photographs of the object are made in the place where it is found and before it is moved in any way. Next the material is cleaned and measured. This allows comparisons to other material from the same or different sites. The data are then analyzed and classified. Often the archaeologist must send material to laboratories for special analyses, such as determining the age of the object or from what it was made. Only after all this work is complete can the archaeologist try to interpret what the excavated material means, what it tells her or him about the past culture.

Context is an absolutely critical concept that archaeologists use in describing and explaining their finds. Context is the information associated

Looters' pits in the Camaná valley of southern Peru. Pieces of cloth, pottery, and human bone litter the area between the holes.

with the object found. For example, a pot is excavated at a particular site. The context of the pot includes other objects that were found with or near it, how close they were to each other, in what kind of soil the pot was found, whether there was anything inside it, whether it was inside some kind of house or other structure. The context is essential to interpreting an object's original use. If a pot was found in a small house, next to a hearth, with the remains of animals and plants around it, it could be interpreted as a cooking vessel. The exact same pot, found carefully buried under the floor of a temple, might be interpreted as an offering to the gods. Finally, the same pot discovered at a burial site could be interpreted as having been placed with the dead person as a possession to be used in the afterlife.

Reread the quote at the beginning of this chapter. Looking at a pot on someone's mantle, one cannot say whether it was used for cooking, as an offering, or as a personal possession. If one is to understand how past cultures lived, it is essential to know the context of the archaeological

Archaeologists excavating a burial in the Netherlands. Preservative has been placed on the bone to harden it prior to removal.

record of that culture. Herein lies the tragedy of looting. Huaqueros do not care about the context of the objects; their sole interest is the object and the money it can bring them. In their haste to dig up treasures, they destroy the context that allows an archaeologist to understand the importance of the object to the people who made and used it.

Who buys looted objects? Individuals who act as middlemen between looters and collectors. Who are those collectors? Often they are wealthy people who want to have beautiful art objects from ancient cultures. Since the 1940s, the art market for antiquities has increased dramatically. Cost is no object. It is not uncommon for gold and silver objects from ancient Andean cultures to command a price of tens of thousands of dollars at auctions (*Plunder!* 1990). Unfortunately for the huaqueros, they receive only a fraction of the ultimate price of an object. Two chains of gold and purple beads looted from a Moche royal burial were sold by looters for $30; the dealer in California who ultimately sold them priced them at $1,500 (Kirkpatrick 1992: 125).

An added ethical issue regarding antiquities is that Peru, like many countries, prohibits either the sale of antiquities or the removal of them from the country. Peruvian law strictly prohibits the export of any objects that are part of the national heritage. Export of such objects is considered smuggling. However, such laws are typically ignored by dealers and collectors anxious to reap the huge profits that such objects can bring. The problem is so great that by 1981 smuggled artifacts were second only to drugs in the amount of money gained illegally (Nagin 1981: 61). It is likely the same is true today.

There is a direct relationship between the growing antiquities market and the destruction of archaeological sites, not just in Peru but everywhere. Because artifacts command such huge prices, collectors of antiquities can pay high prices to the middlemen, who can then pay the huaqueros for the objects. Because most of the high civilizations of the ancient world that created the objects in such demand today existed in countries that are now relatively poor and undeveloped, such as Peru, it is not uncommon that a huaquero can earn two or three months' wages by selling a single pot. To a poor person who has trouble providing food for his family, the motives for looting are strong and perfectly understandable.

A particularly good discussion of the relationship between the antiquities market and the looting of archaeological sites is Sidney Kirkpatrick's *The Lords of Sipán: A Tale of Pre-Inca Tombs, Archaeology, and Crime* (1992). This book documents how huaqueros discovered and looted a rare royal tomb of a Moche lord, and how the artifacts eventually found their way to the southern California art market. It also describes the Peruvian government's efforts to have them returned, and the legal difficulties involved in the question of who owns the objects.

Collectors and dealers are not the only ones to blame. Museums also are often less than careful in verifying the legality of objects they have bought. Thus it is not the huaqueros who are ultimately to blame for the destruction of the world's archaeological resources; it is really the demand for the objects, both private and public.

WHAT CAN BE DONE?

As a result of the problems associated with site looting and its relationship to the antiquities trade, international conventions have been passed to control the trade in antiquities. Unfortunately, differing interpretations of the conventions in individual countries have reduced their utility. For example, the 1970 UNESCO Convention on the Means of Prohibiting and Preventing the Illicit Import, Export, and Transfer of Ownership of Cultural Property was meant to prohibit countries from importing objects stolen from other countries that signed the treaty. However, the U.S. legislation that actually made the principles of the Convention a law stated that for something to be "stolen" it must be proven that it was owned by a specific museum, government agency, or church (Vitelli 1984: 151). Interpretation of this law negated the blanket claim that many Latin American countries, including Peru, had over all objects from their countries. Under this interpretation, many of the objects looted from the royal tombs of Sipán were returned not to Peru, but to the California dealer who then sold them for whatever he wished (Kirkpatrick 1992: 193).

As complicated as the legal issues seem to be, the response by the professional archaeological societies in the United States is clear: all archaeologists should support and comply with the Convention as adopted in 1970, not as legislated by the U.S. Congress in 1983 (Society of Professional Archaeologists 1984: 22–24).

The answer to the problem of archaeological site destruction by looting ultimately must be to reduce the demand (Koczka 1990: 191). But this does not seem likely to occur. In fact, the demand for antiquities continues to increase, and with it, the prices paid. Increased law enforcement in preventing looting does not appear to be a viable option either: the number of officers that would be required to patrol any area of Peru effectively, for example, would be tremendous. Who would pay for such enforcement?

The answer to the looting problem is that everyone must be responsible. It is not enough that we leave the effort of protecting the archaeological resources of the world to policing agencies. It is everyone's duty to do whatever he or she can to help. As Jaime Litvak King, a Mexican archaeologist, has so well stated: "[C]ultural property is not, and cannot be claimed to be the absolute property of a nation, any one nation. It is the property of humankind as a whole since it represents the achievement of a part of all humankind that cannot be set apart from other achievements, in other geographical places" (Litvak King 1990: 199). If such is the case, then it is also our responsibility to preserve humankind's vestiges of the past.

How can this be done? What can the average citizen do to prevent sites from being plundered and destroyed? The first thing is to obey all laws of the country where one lives or visits. In the United States, the principal law that applies is the Archaeological Resources Protection Act (ARPA). This law prohibits the removal or damage, without a permit, of any archaeological resource (such as a site or objects from a site) that is on public or Native American lands. It also prohibits the buying, selling, or exchange of any such materials if they have been illegally obtained. Punishments include fines of $10,000 and/or jail terms of up to one year, more if a person is convicted of the same crime more than once.

In foreign countries, other laws apply and should also be obeyed. In Mexico, Peru, Ecuador, and Guatemala, where all objects are claimed as property by the government, it is illegal to take *any* antiquity out of the country. Tourists are often approached by local people, asking if they would like to buy a "huaca." Although the objects are beautiful and the prices are reasonable, it is against the law to purchase the objects and take them out of the country. And one must remember the reason: when an object is sold, it encourages the looter to go out and dig for more, resulting in further destruction of archaeological sites.

There are other things a person can do besides not buying objects. One of the major problems confronting many national parks in the United States is the accidental or unknowing damage to sites caused by tourists walking where they are not supposed to or climbing on monuments (*Assault on Time* 1992). Although it might be tempting to go to the top of an earthwork at a battlefield, if everyone did so the earthwork might easily be worn down to almost nothing. Similarly, one should never take anything from a national park or archaeological site. It may seem harmless to take as a souvenir a small object such as a musket ball or fragment of pottery, but when many, many people do the same thing, there remains less and less to be appreciated by others—and to be studied by archaeologists for the benefit of everyone.

This last statement includes the so-called harmless act of "collecting arrowheads." Even though it is exciting to find arrowheads (and spear points, pottery, and almost anything else ancient, for that matter), one must remember that every piece of information from a site is valuable and that the context of the piece is as valuable as the object itself. To pick it up and take it away causes a small but significant loss to society's understanding of that site. It is better to simply remember where the site is and report it to an archaeologist. One is usually present at most local colleges and universities.

Another thing everyone can do is join an organization that supports and preserves archaeological sites. Almost every state has an archaeology society that may have local chapters in towns throughout the state. Local chapters often meet once a month or so, providing speakers on topics of interest to its members. In addition, many chapters sponsor archaeological digs in the summer months that provide opportunities to learn how to dig properly and carefully. Digs also provide the opportunity to find things, which is and always has been the most exciting part of archaeology!

Moreover, there are national organizations that promote archaeology. The largest in the United States are the Society for American Archaeology and the Archaeological Institute of America. Both organizations use membership dues for publishing scientific journals (*American Antiquity* and *Latin American Antiquity* by the former, *Archaeology* by the latter) and supporting projects and legislation that protect archaeological resources, in America and throughout the world. Anyone may join either organization. The address of the Society for American Archaeology is 900 Second Street NE #12, Washington, DC 20002-3557 (telephone: 202-789-8260). The address of the Archaeological Institute of America is 656 Beacon Street, Boston, MA 02215-2010 (telephone: 617-353-9361, fax: 617-353-6550, e-mail: aia@bu.edu).

THE CONSEQUENCES OF DOING NOTHING

What are the consequences of doing nothing? The destruction of most, if not all, achaeological sites in the world, probably in our lifetime or certainly in our children's. A study conducted in 1975 indicated that 80 to 90 percent of the sites in Utah's San Juan County were essentially undamaged; but by 1985, only 10 to 20 percent remained undamaged (cited in Koczka 1990: 187). Looting in the Maya area of Central America is so bad that George Stuart, a Maya specialist working for the National Geographic Society, doubts there exists a Maya site that has not been looted to some extent (*Plunder!* 1990). Such stories can be told by archaeologists working in almost every country of the world.

The archaeological record is very incomplete: only a fraction of the objects used by ancient societies are preserved for archaeologists to study. In addition, natural forces such as rivers, streams, and coastlines destroy sites that were located nearby. Many sites become buried by deposits of soil or rock, and thus disappear as well. Hence the total amount of material actually left by a past culture to be studied is reduced to a small fraction. This makes every bit of it valuable.

What if there were no more archaeological sites? We would only know what we have already learned, which is very little. If the rest of the Inca sites were destroyed, there would be no need to update this book in the future, because there would be no new information to provide. We would know only a tiny part of human history, small bits about the exotic and fascinating cultures that preceded us and out of which our own society ultimately developed.

Writing systems are only about 5,000 years old. Therefore, over 99 percent of our cultural development occurred before humans had a way of writing down history for the future. Without archaeology and the sites that are its focus, we would know little of our past development. With regard to this book, we would know something about the Incas from the early Spanish records, but we would not know whether the records are accurate. And we would know nothing of the incredible cultures that existed before the Incas: the Moche, Huari, Nazca, and Chimu, to name but a few.

One of the characteristics of our species is our curiosity about the world. One of the things we all find truly fascinating is our history: where we came from. But the past is fragile, and we must all work to preserve it. The consequence if we don't is an ignorance of the rich heritage of what it means to be human.

Glossary

acllyaconas The Chosen Women, a special class of workers who made cloth, beer, and other products for the empire in special sections of the Inca administrative centers.

adobe Mudbrick.

alpaca One of the domesticated South American members of the camel family, along with the llama. It is bred for its fine wool, which is used in clothing.

Altiplano The high, flat land located around Lake Titicaca in southeastern Peru and northwestern Bolivia.

amautas Teachers at the Inca school for young men in Cuzco. Also a term for any wise man.

Amazonia The vast, low-lying region that forms the basin of the Amazon River. It covers much of north central South America, from the Andes Mountains in the west to the Atlantic Ocean in the east.

Antisuyu The eastern quarter of the Inca empire.

apo The person in charge of one of the quarters of the Inca empire. He was usually a close relative of the king.

archaeology A set of techniques and procedures for reconstructing past cultures from their remains.

artifact Any object made or modified by humans.

aryballos A large storage vessel with pointed base and long flaring neck.

ayllu A group of related individuals and families who exchange labor and cooperate in subsistence and ritual activities.

Aymara   A term for both the language and the indigenous people of the Lake Titicaca area.

Aymoray   The celebration of the corn harvest, held in the modern month of May.

Bering land bridge   The area of the present Bering Strait, which separates eastern Russia from Alaska. During the last ice age this area was a grassy plain because sea levels were lower, which allowed animals, plants, and humans to enter the New World without having to cross a body of water.

callanca   A long rectangular Inca building, often with multiple doors.

cancha   An Inca compound of three or more rectangular buildings surrounding an open patio, all surrounded by a wall.

Capac Raymi   A series of important rituals celebrated during the modern month of December, including the male puberty rites.

ceja de la montaña   The eastern foothills of the Andes in Ecuador and Peru, where the mountains drop into Amazonia. It is a hot, humid, and heavily forested environment.

ceque system   A group of straight lines originating from the Coricancha in Cuzco along which were located important huacas used in the 328-day nighttime calendar.

ceremonial center   A place where people from a wide region assembled on certain sacred days to worship, but which had only a small resident population of priests and their helpers.

Chan Chan   The capital of the Chimu society, located near modern Trujillo.

charqui   Freeze-dried meat.

chasqui   An Inca road system messenger.

Chavin   The name of an art style and the religious cult that is identified by the art style. It dates to the Early Horizon.

chicha   Beer, usually made of corn, but other grains or fruit could be used.

Chimu   A powerful culture that existed on the northern coast of Peru during the Late Intermediate Period. It was famous for its great walled compounds that were both administrative centers and the residence of kings, and for its black pottery.

Chinchaysuyu   The northern quarter of the Inca empire. It and Collasuyu were the largest quarters, in terms of both area and population.

Chosen Women (acllyaconas)   A special class of workers who made cloth, beer, and other products for the empire in special sections of the Inca administrative centers.

chullpas   Funerary buildings, usually in the shape of a two-story tower.

chuño   Freeze-dried potatoes.

ciudadelas   The large walled compounds that housed the Chimu rulers at Chan Chan.

coca A domesticated plant grown for its leaves, which are chewed with lime to reduce feelings of fatigue, hunger, and thirst.

Collasuyu The southern quarter of the Inca empire. It and Chinchaysuyu were the largest quarters, in terms of both area and population.

Conquest Quechua Period The period of time between A.D. 1532–1572 characterized as a time of transition after the Spanish Conquest resulting from the imposition of colonial policies and practices.

conquistadores The Spanish word for "conquerors." Here it refers to the Spaniards under Francisco Pizarro who defeated the Incas.

context The information associated with an object during excavations, including other objects, soil characteristics, and structural remains.

Coricancha The most important temple in Cuzco. It was called the Temple of the Sun, but it housed images of other deities as well.

corregidor A person in charge of a corregimiento.

corregimiento A Spanish colonial policy of the sixteenth and seventeenth century that replaced the encomienda system. The policy placed native labor in the hands of Spanish Crown authorities, rather than private individuals.

coya The wife of the Inca king. In the later years of the empire, she was required to be his full sister.

craft specialization The making of crafts—pottery, jewelry, clothing, ornaments, stone tools, and the like—by specialists, people who do nothing but make that craft.

cumbi The finest grade of cloth.

Cuntisuyu The western quarter of the Inca empire.

curaca An administrative position with responsibility for the control of a certain number of households. There were curacas of groups of 10,000; 5,000; 1,000; 500; and 100 households.

curaca class The middle social echelon of the Inca empire, comprising the curacas and their families.

curers Individuals who claimed to have been contacted by spirits and told how to heal illnesses.

deities Gods.

divination The attempt to foretell events in the future.

division of labor The way in which a society divides the activities of its members: for example, farming, fishing, herding, craft manufacturing, and administering government activities.

domesticated The term used for any animal or plant whose reproduction is controlled by humans.

Early Colonial Period The period between A.D. 1572–1650 when native Andean people had largely adjusted to Spanish rule.

Early Horizon The period between 900 and 200 B.C. in the central Peruvian Andes, when Chavin influence is found at sites in the highlands and along the coast.

Early Intermediate Period   The period between 200 B.C. and A.D. 600 in the central Peruvian Andes, when societies differentiated after the disappearance of the Chavin cult.

economy   The management of a society's resources, including the way people produce and distribute food, raw materials, and manufactured goods.

elites   The highest-status individuals in a society.

encomendero   An individual in charge of an encomienda grant.

encomienda   A Spanish colonial policy of the sixteenth century. It was a grant of native labor to a Spanish colonist.

estate   Lands and associated structures that were owned by a particular Inca person or institution.

extirpation of idolatry   A Spanish colonial policy of the seventeenth century whose purpose was the elimination of all native religious practices.

geoglyph   A drawing scraped onto the surface of the ground.

government   A group of people whose fulltime job is to direct what people do and where goods go in society.

Gran Chaco   A flat, low-lying region east of the Andes Mountains in Bolivia, Paraguay, and Argentina that is dry in the winter and flooded in the summer.

hearth   A fireplace.

Historical Period   The period from A.D. 1532 to the present, when Europeans arrived in the Andes and written records began.

horizon   An archaeological term for a period of time when large areas were unified relatively quickly by a common cultural influence. A horizon is identified by the presence of similar cultural items, such as artifacts or symbols on pottery or buildings, in different areas that all date to roughly the same time.

huaca   A place or object with supernatural forces.

huaquero   A looter of antiquities.

Huari   A powerful culture that spread its authority over much of the Peruvian Andes during the Middle Horizon.

Illapa   The Thunder, or Weather, god of the Incas.

Inca   A term generally referring to the ethnic group that lived in the vicinity of Cuzco and became the dominant political power of the Andes during the Late Horizon. It can also refer to the king (the Inca) or the empire that the ethnic group built.

Inca-by-blood   A term applied to the original Inca group who founded Cuzco.

Inca-by-privilege   A term applied to the ethnic groups of non-Incas who lived near Cuzco and who were given certain privileges of being Inca due to their loyal service to the empire.

Inca class The highest social echelon of the Inca empire that consisted of the Incas and the Inca-by-privilege.

Initial Period The period between 1800 and 900 B.C. in the Peruvian Andes. It is characterized by the appearance of pottery and expanded use of domesticated plants and animals.

institutionalized reciprocity The Inca policy of expecting conquered people to work for them, but in return providing them with services and goods, food and clothing, beer, coca, and even entertainment.

Inti The Sun god of the Incas.

Inti Raymi The festival of the Sun god, Inti, held in the modern month of June.

kaolin A fine, pure white clay used by the Recuay culture in making pottery during the Early Intermediate Period.

Kotosh Religious Tradition A religious belief system of the Preceramic and Initial Periods, represented by rooms with underground ventilation shafts leading to a central hearth, where offerings were burned.

labor class The lowest social echelon in the Inca empire, consisting of the conquered people who did the labor for the Incas.

Late Horizon The period between A.D. 1438 and 1532 in the central Peruvian Andes, when the Incas built their empire.

Late Intermediate Period The time between A.D. 1000 and 1438 in the central Peruvian Andes. It is characterized as a time of cultural differentiation after the decline of the Huari and Tiahuanaco cultures.

llama One of the domesticated South American members of the camel family, along with the alpaca. It is used as a beast of burden.

Llanos de Mojos A flat, low-lying region east of the Andes Mountains in Bolivia, which is dry in the winter and flooded in the summer.

locro A stew made of meat, potatoes, chuño, vegetables, and chili peppers.

Mama-Cocha The Inca goddess of the sea and water.

mamaconas Consecrated women attendants at the Inca temples.

Mama-Quilla The Moon goddess of the Incas.

mamazara The corn deity.

Manco Capac The legendary founder of the Inca people.

manioc A starchy root that is a staple low-altitude crop of many South American peoples.

Middle Horizon The period between A.D. 600 and 1000 in the central Peruvian Andes, marked by the expansion of the Huari and Tiahuanaco political powers.

m'ita The Inca labor tax, time required of all conquered people to work in some capacity for the empire.

mitima People living away from their place of birth; people who had been moved to another area by the Incas for economic or political reasons.

Moche   A powerful society located along the northern coast of Peru during the Early Intermediate Period, famous for their outstanding crafts and their religion based on the sacrifice and drinking of war captives' blood by Moche leaders.

moiety   A division of a society into two parts. Inca ayllus were divided into the upper and lower moieties.

motepatasca   A stew made of corn, herbs, and chili peppers.

myths   Stories or legends concerning people and events in the past, especially those that attempt to explain why the world or a people came to be.

Nasca   A society who lived on the south central coast during the Early Intermediate Period. They are known for their polychrome pottery and geoglyphs (the Nazca Lines).

nomadic   The term for any group that frequently moves during the year.

oca   A domesticated tuber that grows in the puna zone. It is long and narrow, and it comes in several colors.

oracle   A supernatural figure that could answer questions about the future.

Pacha-Mama   The Inca goddess of the earth.

pampa   An extensive, rolling grassland in southern Argentina to the east of the Andes Mountains.

panaca   A corporate group of Incas consisting of all the wives, siblings, and offspring of a former king.

Preceramic Period   The time from when humans entered South America until around 1800 B.C. It is characterized by the exclusive use of stone, wood, and bone tools and the development of domesticated plants and animals. Toward the end of period, temples began to be constructed in areas of Peru.

province   An administrative unit of the Inca empire that usually corresponded to the area occupied by a conquered ethnic group.

puna   The environmental zone lying above 3,500 m (11,500 ft) in altitude. It is a zone of tuber agriculture and herding.

qero   A wooden cup or goblet.

quechua   The environmental zone lying between 1,500 and 3,500 m (5,000 and 11,500 ft) in altitude. It is a temperate zone where many major food crops are grown.

Quechua   The term used for the language of the Incas. The term also applies to an ethnic group who lived north of the Incas prior to the development of their empire.

quinoa   A mid-altitude grain with a high protein content.

quipu   A knotted cord device that was used in Inca accounting.

raised field   A technique for increasing agricultural productivity in areas of swampy soil. Dirt is dug out of a trench and piled onto the adjacent surface, forming a higher area (the field) with a lower area (a canal) next to it.

reducción   A Spanish colonial policy of the sixteenth century under which native people were removed from their traditional villages scattered among the fields and were placed in Spanish-designed settlements.

Sacsahuaman   The huge architectural complex located on an imposing hill to the north of Cuzco.

saya   An administrative unit of the Inca empire, consisting of 10,000 households.

social organization   A term referring to the patterns of behavior governing the interactions between individuals, including who one can marry, where newlyweds will live, how the family is defined, what behavior toward one's in-laws is appropriate, and so on.

sorcerors   Individuals who claimed to be able to speak with spirits, and so were consulted when a person needed supernatural assistance.

Tahuantinsuyu   The Inca term for their empire, the "Land of the Four Quarters."

tambo   A small settlement along the Inca highway used as housing and travelers and for other purposes.

tarwi   A kind of grain grown in the quechua zone.

terrace   An artificially leveled field used to increase agricultural land in steeply sloping areas. The terrace is built by constructing a retaining wall across the slope of the hill, then filling the upslope area with soil until the top surface is level with the top of the wall.

textile   Woven fabric.

Tiahuanaco   A culture of the Early Intermediate Period and Middle Horizon located in Bolivia, south of Lake Titicaca. It is famous for its capital, also called Tiahuanaco, where many stone monuments and gateways have been found. It developed on the basis of raised field agriculture and trade with surrounding regions.

topo   An Inca unit of area corresponding to approximately .8 acre. It was also used as a linear measurement corresponding to a distance of 4.5 miles.

trepanation   The Inca and pre-Inca practice of cutting open the skull to expose the brain. It is likely the purpose was to release evil spirits thought to be present inside the skull.

tuber   A thickening or swelling of an underground part of the root of a plant, for example, potatoes and sweet potatoes.

tupu   A large metal pin used by Inca women to hold a mantle around the shoulders.

ullucu   A domesticated tuber that grows in the puna zone.

ushnu A central platform in an Inca plaza used for ceremonies, as a review stand, or as a meeting place.

Valdivia The earliest pottery-using culture of South America, dating to approximately 3000 B.C. It was located on the Pacific Coast and inland regions of the Santa Elena Peninsula of Ecuador.

Viracocha The highest, most important god of the Incas. He was the Creator of the world.

yanacona Servants and personal attendants of the nobility.

yuca A starchy, low-altitude tuber.

yunga The environmental zone lying below 1,500 m in altitude. It is a warm and dry zone, where irrigation is required for agriculture.

Bibliography

Allen, Catherine. 1988. *The Hold Life Has*. Washington, D.C.: Smithsonian Institution Press.

Alva, Walter. 1988. Discovering the New World's richest unlooted tomb. *National Geographic Magazine* 174(4): 510–549.

———. 1990. New tomb of royal splendor. *National Geographic Magazine* 177(6): 2–15.

Ascher, Marcia, and Robert Ascher. 1981. *Code of the Quipu*. Ann Arbor: University of Michigan Press.

Assault on Time. 1992. Jim Hyde, producer and director. Capitol Heights, Md.: National Audiovisual Center. Videocassette, 35 minutes.

Bauer, Brian. 1992. *The Development of the Inca State*. Austin: University of Texas Press.

Bruhns, Karen O. 1994. *Ancient South America*. Cambridge: Cambridge University Press.

Brush, Stephen. 1977. *Mountain, Field, and Family: The Economy and Human Ecology of an Andean Valley*. Philadelphia: University of Pennsylvania Press.

Burger, Richard L. 1988. Unity and heterogeneity within the Chavin horizon. In *Peruvian Prehistory*, Richard Keatinge, ed., pp. 99–144. Cambridge: Cambridge University Press.

———. 1992. *Chavin and the Origins of Andean Civilization*. New York: Thames and Hudson.

Burger, Richard L., and Lucy Salazar-Burger. 1980. Ritual and religion at Huaricoto. *Archaeology* 33(6): 26–32.

Cleere, Henry F. (ed.). 1989. *Archaeological Heritage Management in the Modern World*. London: Unwin Hyman.

Cobo, Bernabé. 1890–1895 [1653]. *Historia del Nuevo Mundo*, 4 vols. Published for the first time with notes and other illustrations by Don Marcos Jiménez de la Espada. Sociedad de Bibliófilos, Andaluces, Sevilla.

———. 1979 [1653]. *History of the Inca Empire.* Translated and edited by Roland Hamilton. Austin: University of Texas Press.

———. 1990. *Inca Religion and Customs.* Translated and edited by Roland Hamilton. Austin: University of Texas Press.

Conrad, Geoffrey, and Arthur Demarest. 1984. *Religion and Empire: The Dynamics of Aztec and Inca Expansion.* New York: Cambridge University Press.

Cook, David Noble. 1981. *Demographic Collapse: Peru, 1520–1620.* Cambridge: Cambridge University Press.

D'Altroy, Terence. 1992. *Provincial Power in the Inca Empire.* Washington, D.C.: Smithsonian Institution Press.

Day, Kent C. 1982. Ciudadelas: Their form and function. In *Chan Chan: Andean Desert City,* Michael E. Moseley and Kent C. Day, eds., pp. 55–66. Albuquerque: University of New Mexico Press, School of American Research.

Dearborn, David S. P., and Katharina J. Schreiber. 1989. Houses of the rising sun. In *Time and Calendars in the Inca Empire,* Mariusz S. Ziolkowski and Robert M. Sadowski, eds., pp. 49–74. Oxford: British Archaeological Reports, International Series 479.

Denevan, William. 1987. Terrace abandonment in the Colca Valley, Peru. In *Pre-Hispanic Agricultural Fields in the Andean Region,* William M. Denevan, Kent Mathewson, and Gregory Knapp, eds., pp. 1–44. Oxford: British Archaeological Reports, International Series 359(i).

Denevan, William M., Kent Mathewson, and Gregory Knapp (eds.). 1987. *Pre-Hispanic Agricultural Fields in the Andean Region.* Oxford: British Archaeological Reports, International Series 359.

Donnan, Christopher (ed.). 1985. *Early Ceremonial Architecture in the Andes.* Washington, D.C.: Dumbarton Oaks.

———. 1988. Unraveling the mystery of the Warrior Priest. *National Geographic Magazine* 174(4): 550–555.

———. 1990. Masterworks of art reveal a remarkable pre-Inca world. *National Geographic Magazine* 177(6): 16–33.

Earle, Timothy, Terence D'Altroy, Christine Hastorf, Catherine Scott, Cathy Costin, Glen Russell, and Elsie Sandefur. 1987. *Archaeological Field Research in the Upper Mantaro, Peru, 1982–1983: Investigations of Inka Expansion and Exchange.* Los Angeles: University of California–Los Angeles, Institute of Archaeology, Monograph XXVIII.

Erickson, Clark. 1988. Raised field agriculture in the Lake Titicaca basin. *Expedition* 30(3): 8–16.

Feldman, Robert. 1987. Architectural evidence for the development of nonegalitarian social systems in coastal Peru. In *The Origins and Development of the Andean State,* Jonathan Haas, Sheila Pozorski, and Thomas Pozorski, eds., pp. 9–14. Cambridge: Cambridge University Press.

Garcilaso de la Vega, El Inga. 1966 [1609]. *Royal Commentaries of the Incas and General History of Peru, Parts 1 and 2.* Translated by Harold V. Livermore. Austin: University of Texas Press.

Gasparini, Graziano, and Luise Margolis. 1980. *Inca Architecture.* Bloomington: Indiana University Press.

Green, Ernestene L. (ed.). 1984. *Ethics and Values in Archaeology.* New York: Free Press.

Grosboll, Sue. 1987. Ethnic boundaries within the Inca empire. In *Ethnicity in Complex Societies,* Reginald Auger, Margaret F. Glass, Scott MacEachern, and Peter H. McCartney, eds., pp. 115–125. Calgary: Archaeological Association of the University of Calgary, Alberta.

———. 1993. . . . And he said in the time of the Ynga, they paid tribute and served the Ynga. In *Provincial Inca,* Michael A. Malpass, ed., pp. 44–76. Iowa City: University of Iowa Press.

Guaman Poma de Ayala, Felipe. 1936. *Nueva Corónica y Buen Gobierno (Codex Péruvien illustré).* Paris: Institut d'Ethnologie, Travaux et Mémoires, Vol. 23.

———. 1980. *El Primer Nueva Corónica y Buen Gobierno [1584–1615],* John V. Murra and Rolena Adorno, eds. Translated by Jorge I. Urioste. 3 vols. Mexico City: Siglo Ventiuno.

Hanna, Joel. 1976. Drug use. In *Man in the Andes: A Multidisciplinary Study of the High-Altitude Quechua,* Paul Baker and Michael Little, eds., pp. 363–378. Stroudsburg, Pa.: Dowden, Hutchinson, and Ross.

Hyslop, John. 1984. *The Inka Road System.* New York: Academic Press.

———. 1990. *Inka Settlement Planning.* Austin: University of Texas Press.

The Incas. 1979. Anna Bensongyles, producer. PBS Video, Odyssey series. Videocassette, 55 minutes.

Isbell, William H. 1993. Huari administration and the orthogonal cellular architecture horizon. In *Huari Administrative Structure,* William H. Isbell and Gordon F. McEwan, eds., pp. 293–316. Washington, D.C.: Dumbarton Oaks.

Isbell, William H., and Gordon F. McEwan (eds.). 1993. *Huari Administrative Structure.* Washington, D.C.: Dumbarton Oaks.

Jennings, Jesse (ed.). 1983. *Ancient South Americans.* San Francisco: W. H. Freeman and Company.

Julien, Catherine. 1982. Inca decimal administration in the Lake Titicaca region. In *The Inca and Aztec States, 1400–1800: Anthropology and History,* George A. Collier, Renato I. Rosaldo, and John D. Wirth, eds., pp. 119–151. New York: Academic Press.

———. 1988. How Inca decimal administration worked. *Ethnohistory* 35 (3): 257–297.

———. 1993. Finding a fit: Archaeology and ethnohistory of the Incas. In *Provincial Inca,* Michael A. Malpass, ed., pp. 177–233. Iowa City: University of Iowa Press.

Keatinge, Richard (ed.). 1988. *Peruvian Prehistory.* Cambridge: Cambridge University Press.

Kendall, Ann. 1973. *Everyday Life of the Incas.* New York: G.P. Putnam and Sons.

Kirkpatrick, Sydney D. 1992. *Lords of Sipán: A Tale of Pre-Inca Tombs, Archaeology, and Crime.* New York: William Morrow and Company.

Klymyshyn, Ulana. 1982. Elite compounds in Chan Chan. In *Chan Chan: Andean Desert City,* Michael E. Moseley and Kent C. Day, eds., pp. 119–144. Albuquerque: University of New Mexico Press, School of American Research.

Koczka, Charles. 1990. The need for enforcing regulations on the international art trade. In *The Ethics of Collecting Cultural Property*, Phyllis Mauch Messenger, ed., pp. 185–198. Albuquerque: University of New Mexico Press.

Kolata, Alan L. 1983. The South Andes. In *Ancient South Americans*, Jesse Jennings, ed., pp. 241–286. San Francisco: W. H. Freeman and Company.

Kubler, George. 1946. The Quechua in the colonial world. In *Handbook of South American Indians, Vol. 2. The Andean Civilizations*, Julian H. Steward, ed., pp. 331–410. Washington, D.C.: Bureau of American Ethnology, Bulletin 143.

Lathrap, Donald. 1977. Our father the cayman, our mother the gourd: Spinden revisited, or a unitary model for the emergence of agriculture in the New World. In *Origins of Agriculture*, Charles A. Reed, ed., pp. 713–752. The Hague: Mouton.

Lettau, Heinz, and Katharina Lettau (eds.). 1978. *Exploring the World's Driest Climate*. Madison: University of Wisconsin–Madison, Institute for Environmental Studies, Report 101.

Litvak King, Jaime. 1990. Cultural property and national sovereignty. In *The Ethics of Collecting Cultural Property*, Phyllis Mauch Messenger, ed., pp. 199–208. Albuquerque: University of New Mexico Press.

Lynch, Thomas F. 1980. *Guitarrero Cave: Early Man in the Andes*. New York: Academic Press.

———. 1993. The identification of Inca posts and roads from Catarpe to Río Frío, Chile. In *Provincial Inca*, Michael A. Malpass, ed., pp. 117–144. Iowa City: University of Iowa Press.

Malpass, Michael A. 1987. Prehistoric agricultural terracing at Chijra in the Colca Valley, Peru: Preliminary report II. In *Pre-Hispanic Agricultural Fields in the Andean Region*, William M. Denevan, Kent Mathewson, and Gregory Knapp, ed., pp. 45–66. Oxford: British Archaeological Reports, International Series 359(i).

———. 1993a. Provincial Inca archaeology and ethnohistory: An introduction. In *Provincial Inca*, Michael A. Malpass, ed., pp. 1–16. Iowa City: University of Iowa Press.

——— (ed.). 1993b. *Provincial Inca*. Iowa City: University of Iowa Press.

McGimsey, Charles R. III. 1972. *Public Archeology*. New York: Seminar Press.

Messenger, Phyllis Mauch (ed.). 1989. *The Ethics of Collecting Cultural Property*. Albuquerque: University of New Mexico Press.

Meyer, Karl. 1973. *The Plundered Past*. New York: Atheneum.

Mishkin, Bernard. 1946. The contemporary Quechua. In *Handbook of South American Indians, Vol. 2. The Andean Civilizations*, Julian H. Steward, ed., pp. 411–500. Washington, D.C.: Bureau of American Ethnology, Bulletin 143.

Morris, Craig. 1978. The archaeological study of Andean exchange systems. In *Social Archaeology: Beyond Subsistence and Dating*, Charles Redman, Marc J. Bermann, E. V. Curtin, William T. Langhorne, Nina M. Versaggi, and J. C. Wagner, eds., pp. 315–327. New York: Academic Press.

Morris, Craig, and Donald E. Thompson. 1985. *Huánuco Pampa: An Inca City and Its Hinterland*. New York: Thames and Hudson.

Morris, Craig, and Adriana von Hagen. 1993. *The Inka Empire and Its Andean*

Origins. New York: American Museum of Natural History and Abbeville Press.

Morúa, Martín de. 1922–1925. *Historia del Orígen y Genealogía de los Reyes Incas del Perú, de sus Hechos, Costumbres, Trajes y Manera de Gobierno,* H. H. Urteaga and C. A. Romero, eds., Colección de Libros y Documentos Referentes a la Historia del Perú, 2nd series; Vol. 4: 1–253, vol. 5: 1–72. Lima, Peru.

Moseley, Michael E. 1975. *Maritime Foundations of Andean Civilization.* Menlo Park, Calif.: Cummings Publishing Company.

———. 1992. *The Incas and Their Ancestors.* New York: Thames and Hudson.

Murra, John V. 1962. Cloth and its functions in the Inca state. *American Anthropologist* 64: 710–728.

———. 1972. El "control vertical" de un maximo de pisos ecológicos en la economía de las sociedades Andinas. In *Visita de la provincia de León de Huánuco,* Iñigo Ortíz de Zúñiga, Vol. 2: 429–476. Huánuco: Universidad Nacional Hermilio Valizán.

———. 1975. *Formaciones Económicas y Políticas del Mundo Andino.* Lima: Instituto de Estudios Peruanos.

Nagin, C. 1981. First, the "Hot Pot"—Now, the "Uncup." *New York,* December 7: 61–74.

Niles, Susan. 1987. *Callachaca: Style and Status in an Inca Community.* Iowa City: University of Iowa Press.

———. 1993. The provinces in the heartland: Stylistic variation and architectural innovation near Inca Cuzco. In *Provincial Inca,* Michael A. Malpass, ed., pp. 145–176. Iowa City: University of Iowa Press.

Pease, Franklin G. Y. (ed.). 1977. *Collaguas I.* Lima: Pontificia Universidad Católica del Peru.

Plunder! 1990. Jim Gilmore, producer and director. ABC News Frontline series. Washington, D.C.: PBS Videos. Videocassette, 60 minutes.

Pozorski, Sheila, and Thomas Pozorski. 1987. *Early Settlement and Subsistence in the Casma Valley, Peru.* Iowa City: University of Iowa Press.

Reinhard, Johan. 1992. Sacred peaks of the Andes. *National Geographic Magazine* 181(3): 86–111.

Root, William C. 1949. Metallurgy. In *Handbook of South American Indians, Vol. 5. Comparative Ethnology of South American Indians,* Julian H. Steward, ed., pp. 205–226. Washington, D.C.: Bureau of American Ethnology, Bulletin 143.

Rowe, John H. 1946. Inca culture at the time of the Spanish conquest. In *Handbook of South American Indians, Vol. 2. The Andean Civilizations,* Julian H. Steward, ed., pp. 183–330. Washington, D.C.: Bureau of American Ethnology, Bulletin 143.

———. 1967. What kind of a settlement was Inca Cuzco? *Ñawpa Pacha* 5: 59–76.

———. 1982. Inca policies and institutions relating to the unification of the empire. In *The Inca and Aztec States, 1400–1800: Anthropology and History,* George A. Collier, Renato I. Rosaldo, and John D. Wirth, eds., pp. 93–118. New York: Academic Press.

Sadowski, Robert M. 1989. A few remarks on the astronomy of R. T. Zuidema's "quipu-calendar." In *Time and Calendars in the Inca Empire,* Mariusz S.

Ziolkowski and Robert M. Sadowski, eds., pp. 209–213. Oxford: British Archaeological Reports, International Series 479.

Salomon, Frank. 1986. *Native Lords of Quito in the Age of the Incas.* Cambridge: Cambridge University Press.

Sandweiss, Daniel, James B. Richardson III, Elizabeth Reitz, Jeffrey Hsu, and Robert Feldman. 1989. Early maritime adaptations in the Andes: Preliminary studies at the Ring site, Peru. In *Ecology, Settlement and History in the Osmore Drainage, Peru,* Don S. Rice, Charles Stanish, and Phillip R. Scarr, eds., pp. 35–84. Oxford: British Archaeological Reports, International Series 545.

Schreiber, Katharina. 1992. *Wari Imperialism in Middle Horizon Peru.* Ann Arbor: University of Michigan Museum of Anthropology, Anthropological Paper 87.

———. 1993. The Inca occupation of the province of Andamarca Lucanas, Peru. In *Provincial Inca,* Michael A. Malpass, ed., pp. 77–116. Iowa City: University of Iowa Press.

Schreiber, Katharina, and Josué Lamuho Rojas. 1995. The puquois of Nasca. *Latin American Antiquity* 6(3): 229–254.

Silverblatt, Irene. 1987. *Moon, Sun, and Witches.* Princeton: Princeton University Press.

Silverman, Helaine. 1990. The early Nasca pilgrimage center of Cahuachi and the Nazca lines: Anthropological and archaeological perspectives. In *The Lines of Nazca,* Anthony Aveni, ed., pp. 209–304. Philadelphia: American Philosophical Society.

Smith, Bruce D. 1994–1995. The origins of agriculture in the Americas. *Evolutionary Anthropology* 3(5): 174–184.

Society of Professional Archaeologists. 1984. Code of Ethics. In *Ethics and Values in Archaeology,* Ernestene L. Green, ed., pp. 22–24. New York: The Free Press.

Squier, E. George. 1877. *Peru: Incidents of Travel and Exploration in the Land of the Incas.* New York: Harper.

Topic, John R. 1982. Lower-class social and economic organization at Chan Chan. In *Chan Chan: Andean Desert City,* Michael E. Moseley and Kent C. Day, eds., pp. 145–175. Albuquerque: University of New Mexico Press, School of American Research.

Topic, John R., and Theresa Lange Topic. 1993. A summary of the Inca occupation of Huamachuco. In *Provincial Inca,* Michael A. Malpass, ed., pp. 17–43. Iowa City: University of Iowa Press.

Ulloa Mogollón, Juan de. 1965 [1586]. Relación de la provincia de los Collaguas. In *Relaciones Geográficas de Indias (Peru),* Don Marcos Jiménez de la Espada, ed., Vol. 183: 326–333. Madrid: Ediciones Atlas, Biblioteca de Autores Españoles.

Urton, Gary. 1990. *The History of a Myth.* Austin: University of Texas Press.

Vitelli, Karen D. 1984. The international traffic in antiquities: Archaeological ethics and the archaeologist's responsibility. In *Ethics and Values in Archaeology,* Ernestene L. Green, ed., pp. 143–155. New York: Free Press.

Ziolkowsi, Mariusz S. 1989. Knots and kinks. The quipu-calendar or supposed Cuzco luni-sidereal calendar. In *Time and Calendars in the Inca Empire,*

Mariusz S. Ziolkowski and Robert M. Sadowski, eds., pp. 197–208. Oxford: British Archaeological Reports, International Series 479.

Ziolkowsi, Mariusz S., and Robert M. Sadowski (eds.). 1989. *Time and Calendars in the Inca Empire*. Oxford: British Archaeological Reports, International Series 479.

Zuidema, R. Thomas 1964. *The Ceque System of Cuzco: The Social Organization of the Capital of the Inca*. Leiden: E. J. Brill.

———. 1982. The sidereal lunar calendar of the Incas. In *Archaeoastronomy in the New World*, Anthony Aveni, ed., pp. 59–107. Cambridge: Cambridge University Press.

———. 1983. Hierarchy and space in incaic social organization. *Ethnology* 30(2): 49–75.

———. 1990. *Inca Civilization in Cuzco*. Translated by Jean-Jacques Decoster. Austin: University of Texas Press.

PHOTOGRAPH AND ILLUSTRATION SOURCES

Introduction

Both figures from Guaman Poma (1980).

Chapter 1

All photographs—except the sunken circular court at Salinas de Chao, the Moche vessel, and the Staff God from the Gateway of the Sun at Tiahuanaco—by the author. The photograph of the sunken circular court at Salinas de Chao is by Thomas and Sheila Pozorski; the photograph of the Staff God is by Lars Fogelin. The photograph of the Moche vessel is by Donald Proulx; the vessel, UCHMA 4-2712, is used with permission of the Phoebe A. Hearst Museum of Anthropology, University of California, Berkeley. Figure of the Kotosh ceremonial room, Nasca geoglyph, and field system by the author. Figure of Huaca A storage facility by Thomas and Sheila Pozorski. Figure of Atahuallpa and Pizarro from Guaman Poma (1980).

Chapter 2

Photographs of the Inca stonework and Sacsahuaman by the author. All figures from Guaman Poma (1980). Table by the author.

Chapter 3

All figures from Guaman Poma (1980).

Chapter 5

Figure from Guaman Poma (1980).

Chapter 7

Photographs by the author. Figure from Guaman Poma (1980).

Chapter 8

Photographs by the author.

Index

About the Author

MICHAEL A. MALPASS is Associate Professor of Anthropology at Ithaca College in Ithaca, New York. He has been actively engaged in archaeological research in Peru since 1980. His research interests include the early occupations of western South America, the evolution of agricultural systems in the Andes, the Huari state, and the impact of the Inca state on Andean people. He is the author of *Provincial Inca: Archaeological and Ethnohistorical Assessment of the Impact of the Inca State* (1993).